Pastoral, insightful, and significant, Dan Ebert's *Wisdom Christology* expounds key truths about Christ, clarifies how Christ is the wisdom of God, and displays how Christology often functions as wisdom in the New Testament. Ebert models how careful exegesis grounds sound theology and shows how sound theology must be applied—to the church and for the church.

—Christopher W. Morgan, California Baptist University

Two features of this book merit particular praise. First, negatively, Ebert carefully demolishes the "Jesus as Lady Sophia" Christology that dominates far too many books; and second, positively, Ebert fulsomely displays how true wisdom is rightly connected to Jesus Christ. Moreover, the author writes well. I hope this book will be read by many.

—D. A. Carson, Trinity Evangelical Divinity School

A fascinating biblical-theological study. Ebert demonstrates persuasively how Wisdom, a central Old Testament theme, played a constraining role in the apostolic era's first-order question, "Who is Jesus?" This is no detached study. Rather, it is a gentle yet prophetic word for believers to coordinate their lives with the wisdom offered in Christ; or better, with the Wisdom who is Christ! I heartily and gratefully recommend it.

—Mark S. Gignilliat, Beeson Divinity School

Dan Ebert reveals the intimate connections between two key biblical motifs, teaching about Jesus Christ and wisdom. By doing so, he helps us better understand the nature of our Lord and what it means to be wise. His book is a marvelous example of biblical theology and shows how that biblical theology informs the way we are to live as God's people in the twenty-first century. It is grounded in solid research yet very accessible.

—Douglas J. Moo, Wheaton College

Praise for the Explorations in Biblical Theology series

Neither superficial nor highly technical, this new series of volumes on important Christian doctrines is projected to teach Reformed theology as it is most helpfully taught, with clear grounding in Scripture, mature understanding of theology, gracious interaction with others who disagree, and useful application to life. I expect that these volumes will strengthen the faith and biblical maturity of all who read them, and I am happy to recommend them highly.

—Wayne Grudem, Phoenix Seminary

There are many misconceptions today about systematic, biblical, and applicatory theology. One sometimes gets the impression that these are opposed to one another, and that the first two, at least, are so obscure that ordinary people should avoid them like the plague. The series Explorations in Biblical Theology seeks to correct these misunderstandings, to bring these disciplines together in a winsome, clear unity, edifying to non-specialists. The authors are first-rate, and they write to build up our faith by pointing us to Christ. That's what biblical and systematic theology at their best have always done, and the best application of Scripture has always shown us in practical ways how to draw on the rich blessings of Jesus' salvation. I hope that many will read these books and take them to heart.

—John Frame, Reformed Theological Seminary

The message of a God who loved us before he formed the earth, called us his own before we could respond to him, died for us while we were dead in our transgressions and sins, made us alive when we were incapable of serving him, unites us to himself so that we can be forever holy, and now loves us more than we love ourselves—sparked a Reformation of hope and joy that transformed the world of faith. Re-declaring that hope and reclaiming that joy is the ambition and delight of this series. Able and godly scholars trace the golden thread of grace that unites all Scripture to make the wonders of our God's redeeming love shine and win hearts anew. The writing is warm, winsome, and respectful of those who differ. The motives are clearly to reveal truth and expose error by glorifying the message and manner of the Savior.

—Bryan Chapell, Covenant Theological Seminary

The aim of these volumes is clear: as regards God's Word, rigor; as regards other scholars, respect; as regards current issues, relevance; as regards the Lord himself, reverence. Effective witness and ministry currently require more than extra effort and better methods: the call is heard from churches across the board for renewal in our grasp of Christian truth. Each author in this series contributes admirably to that urgent need.

—Robert W. Yarbrough, Trinity Evangelical Divinity School

This is a series that the church needs more than ever, as we forge fresh links between the world of biblical studies and our Reformed theology. The contributors remind us again that the Bible is a book about God and his purposes and encourages us to preach and teach the message of salvation which it contains. It will be an inspiration to many and will give us new insight into the faith once delivered to the saints.

—Gerald Bray, Beeson Divinity School

The church of Jesus Christ faces massive cultural challenges today. More and more people in the Western world are ignorant of or hostile to the Christian faith. The moral fabric of our society is unraveling, and as a result of postmodernism many are adopting a relativistic worldview. Some Christians have responded by trying to simplify and dumb down the gospel. Others have tried to catch the cultural mood of the day in order to gain more converts, but they have often been co-opted by the culture instead of transforming it for Christ. What we truly need is to dig down deep into biblical foundations, so that our theology is robustly biblical. Only a worldview that is informed by both biblical and systematic theology can withstand the intellectual challenges that face us today. The series Explorations in Biblical Theology is designed to meet this very need. I commend these volumes enthusiastically, for they explain what the Scriptures teach from the standpoint of biblical theology. What we desperately need to hear and learn today is the whole counsel of God. This series advances that very agenda for the edification of the church and to the glory of God.

—**Thomas R. Schreiner**, The Southern Baptist Theological Seminary

Explorations in Biblical Theology is a valuable new series of books on doctrinal themes that run through Scripture. The contributors are competent scholars who love to serve the church and have special expertise in the Bible and its theology. Following a thematic approach, each volume explores a distinctive doctrine as it is taught in Scripture, or else introduces the various doctrines taught in a particular book of the Bible. The result is a fresh and unique contribution to our understanding of the Bible's own theology.

—**Philip Ryken,** Wheaton College

Explorations in Biblical Theology is a gift to God's people. Biblical theology was never meant to be reserved for academics. When the verities of the Reformed faith are taken from the "ivy halls" of academia and placed in the hearts and minds of the covenant people of God, reformation and revival are the inevitable result. I believe God will use this series as a mighty tool for the Kingdom.

—**Steve Brown,** Reformed Theological Seminary

Wisdom Christology

Explorations in Biblical Theology

*Election and Free Will: God's Gracious Choice
and Our Responsibility*

*Anointed with the Spirit and Power:
The Holy Spirit's Empowering Presence*

The Nearness of God: His Presence with His People

Our Secure Salvation: Preservation and Apostasy

The Elder: Today's Ministry Rooted in All of Scripture

A Theology of James: Wisdom for God's People

Wisdom Christology: How Jesus Becomes God's Wisdom for Us

Robert A. Peterson, series editor

Wisdom Christology

How Jesus Becomes God's Wisdom for Us

Daniel J. Ebert IV

PUBLISHING
P.O. BOX 817 • PHILLIPSBURG • NEW JERSEY 08865-0817

© 2011 by Daniel J. Ebert IV

All rights reserved. No part of this book may be reproduced, stored in a retrieval system, or transmitted in any form or by any means—electronic, mechanical, photocopy, recording, or otherwise—except for brief quotations for the purpose of review or comment, without the prior permission of the publisher, P&R Publishing Company, P.O. Box 817, Phillipsburg, New Jersey 08865–0817.

Unless otherwise indicated, all Scripture quotations are from The Holy Bible, English Standard Version, copyright © 2001 by Crossway, a publishing ministry of Good News Publishers. Used by permission. All rights reserved.

Italics within Scripture quotations indicate emphasis added.

Printed in the United States of America

Library of Congress Cataloging-in-Publication Data

Ebert, Daniel J., 1952-
  Wisdom Christology : how Jesus becomes God's wisdom for us / Daniel J. Ebert IV.
      p. cm. -- (Explorations in Biblical theology)
  Includes bibliographical references and indexes.
  ISBN 978-1-59638-102-5 (pbk.)
  1. Jesus Christ--Person and offices--Biblical teaching. 2. Wisdom--Biblical teaching. 3. Bible. N.T.--Theology. 4. Reformed Church--Doctrines. I. Title. II. Series.

  BT205.E24 2011
  232'.8--dc22

                                                  2011003917

I dedicate this book to my wife,
Sue

"She is far more precious than jewels.
. . . .
She opens her hand to the poor
and reaches out her hands to the needy.
. . . .
She opens her mouth with *wisdom*,
. . . .
She looks well to the ways of her household
. . . .
Her children rise up and call her blessed;
her husband also, and he praises her:
. . . .
A woman who fears the LORD is to be praised."
(Prov. 31:10, 20, 26–28, 30)

Contents

Series Introduction

BELIEVERS TODAY need high-quality literature that attracts them to good theology and builds them up in their faith. Currently, readers may find several sets of lengthy—and rather technical—books on Reformed theology, as well as some that are helpful and semipopular. Explorations in Biblical Theology takes a more mid-range approach, seeking to offer readers the substantial content of the more lengthy books, while striving for the readability of the semipopular books.

This series includes two types of books: (1) some treating biblical themes and (2) others treating the theology of specific biblical books. The volumes dealing with biblical themes seek to cover the whole range of Christian theology, from the doctrine of God to last things. Representative early offerings in the series focus on the empowering by the Holy Spirit, justification, the presence of God, preservation and apostasy, and substitutionary atonement. Examples of works dealing with the theology of specific biblical books are volumes on the theology of 1 and 2 Samuel, Psalms, and Isaiah in the Old Testament, and books on the theology of Mark, Romans, and James in the New Testament.

Explorations in Biblical Theology is written for college seniors, seminarians, pastors, and thoughtful lay readers. These volumes are intended to be accessible and not obscured by excessive references to Hebrew, Greek, or theological jargon.

Each book seeks to be solidly Reformed in orientation, because the writers love the Reformed faith. The various theological themes and biblical books are treated from the perspective of biblical theology. Writers either trace doctrines through the Bible or open up the theology of the specific book they treat. Writers desire not merely to dispense the Bible's good information, but also to apply that information to real needs today.

Explorations in Biblical Theology is committed to being warm and winsome, with a focus on applying God's truth to life. Authors aim to treat those with whom they disagree as they themselves would want to be treated. The motives for the rejection of error are not to fight, hurt, or wound, but to protect, help, and heal. The authors of this series are godly, capable scholars with a commitment to Reformed theology and a burden to minister that theology clearly to God's people.

ROBERT A. PETERSON
Series Editor

Acknowledgments

I WANT TO THANK those who helped bring this book to fruition.

The many students over the years who engaged with my lectures on Christology, especially at the Center for Biblical Studies in the Philippines; at Clearwater Christian College in Florida; at Central Baptist Theological Seminary in Virginia Beach; and at Cedarville University.

My friends, colleagues, and former students, who read the manuscript and offered helpful comments: Sue Ebert, Sharon Moore, Tony Abel, Bill Ebert, Gail Milliman, Heidi Satterberg, and Paul Conrad.

Dorothy Carroll for proofreading and editing the manuscript; Beth Ann Brown and Aaron Hanbury for their editorial help.

My friends at Beans-n-Cream, who served endless cups of coffee and provided my favorite writing environment.

Chris Morgan, who offered valuable counsel both editorially and theologically.

And last but not least, to my editor, Robert Peterson, who for many years has been a teacher, a writing mentor, a friend, and most of all a faithful Christian brother.

Introduction: The Need for Wisdom

ANDREW DELBANCO, in *The Real American Dream*, describes the spiritual history of the United States in three chapters: "God," "Nation," and "Self." In Puritan New England, according to his analysis, the self stretched toward the vastness of God. From the rise of democracy until the Great Society of the 1960s, people turned more and more to a national ideal less than God but larger than any individual citizen. Now, Delbanco writes, "hope has narrowed to the vanishing point of the self alone."[1] The historical divisions, of course, are too neat; there are some wonderful counterexamples of God's grace and goodness in the world today. But the indictment is telling: the story of contemporary culture centers largely on the self.

Today this destructive narrative lures the church; it threatens to turn us and our children into "'black holes of self-absorption': manipulating, cheating, deceiving, and exploiting others."[2] We have all felt its demonic pull. This self-centered wisdom permeates our culture and subtly woos us into its ways. It is not the voice of true wisdom, but of folly.

While this destructive voice sings a contemporary song, its message is not new. The book of Proverbs teaches that "the woman Folly is loud; she is seductive and knows nothing" (Prov. 9:13). In the early church, Jesus' brother James described such thinking

---

1. Andrew Delbanco, *The Real American Dream: A Meditation on Hope* (Cambridge, MA: Harvard University Press, 2000), 103.
2. Miroslav Volf, *Against the Tide: Love in a Time of Petty Dreams and Persisting Enmities* (Grand Rapids: Eerdmans, 2010), xi.

as earthly and unspiritual, characterized by bitter envy, selfish ambition, disorder, and evil (James 3:14–16).

God offers us an alternative wisdom. It "cries aloud" and promises, "If you turn at my reproof, behold, I will pour out my spirit to you; I will make my words known to you" (Prov. 1:20, 23). James describes this wisdom as pure, peace-loving, gentle, submissive, full of mercy and good fruit, impartial, and sincere. It is marked by humility and belongs to those who seek peace (James 3:13, 17–18).

Although seldom noticed, the heavenly wisdom James recommends is thoroughly Christological.[3] His description of wisdom echoes the deepest insights found in what the rest of the New Testament confesses about Christ. There is a profound sense in which wisdom and Christology belong together. In the words of the apostle Paul, Jesus is "wisdom from God" for us (1 Cor. 1:30).

In this book we explore, through the study of selected New Testament passages, how the doctrine of Christ functioned as wisdom for the early church. We need to tune our ears to this wisdom. It is our best hope "to counter the multiple manifestations of human self-absorption and to connect human beings with what ultimately matters—God, whom we should love with all our being, and neighbors, whom we should love as ourselves."[4]

To prepare us to explore this fascinating and important interface between wisdom and Christology, we begin by considering several introductory matters:

- Reasons to Study Christology
- The Focus on Christ as Wisdom
- Preliminary Questions
- A Warning for the Journey

3. "Christology" is a word commonly used in theology to refer to the study of the person and work of Christ. "Christological" is the adjective, and means "related to Christ."

4. Volf, *Against the Tide*, 110.

Reasons to Study Christology

The vitality of our Christian lives, our families, and our churches depends on how we understand and follow Christ. One writer put it this way: "Christianity stands or falls by the adequacy or otherwise of its Christology."[5] There are four specific reasons why we need a deeper understanding of Christ.

First, as the apostle John reminds us, a full account of the person and work of Jesus is inexhaustible (John 21:25). There are depths to Christ that we have not yet discovered. One aspect of Christology that awaits further study is its function in the New Testament as wisdom.

A second reason for exploring Christology is its impact on the health of the church. The church constantly needs to be renewed in the light of both the written and living Word of God. The traditional Reformed motto about the church is true: "the church reformed and always to be reformed."[6] In every age there are characteristics of the church that need to be reshaped by Christological wisdom. The antidote for the unhealthy habits of thought and practice that have infiltrated our churches is the wisdom found in Christ.

Third, our understanding of God's ways must never be stagnant. Scripture is unchanging, and Jesus is the same yesterday, today, and forever. There is an important stability to the basic confession of the Christian faith (Eph. 4:14; Heb. 13:9; Jude 3). But, at the same time, our theological constructs, our human reflection on God and his Word, must constantly be refreshed. There are two questions we must persistently ask if our faith is to remain vital. What does it mean for me to follow Christ in my life, in this time, and in this place? And what does it mean for us today to be his church in the world? The answers to these questions come in the shape of God's wisdom in Christ.

5. Colin Greene, *Christology in Cultural Perspective: Marking Out the Horizons* (Grand Rapids: Eerdmans, 2004), 96.
6. The Latin of this saying often added the key phrase "by the Word of God" (*ecclesia reformata, semper reformanda secundum verbi Dei*).

Fourth, the study of Jesus is for our good and God's glory. The Father is pleased when much is made of his Son. As we will see, the study of the doctrine of Christ leads us to the heart of God's triune life, where we must bow and worship Father, Son, and Spirit. Here, wonder of wonders, through Christ and his wisdom, we come to participate in the very life of God (2 Peter 1:3–4)!

The Focus on Christ as Wisdom

Scattered throughout the New Testament are concentrated Christological passages that reflect a set of themes confessed about Jesus by the earliest church. These joyful celebrations of Christ lead us in a unique way to God's wisdom. The biblical authors apply a set of Christological motifs to the various circumstances of the early church, and to the practical problems the church faced. As a result, these texts model for us how to live in the wisdom of Christ. This study will examine several of these passages to seek this pattern of wisdom.

This focus on the wisdom of Christ cannot be separated from two other questions often discussed in New Testament scholarship. First, did Jesus fulfill the role of a wisdom teacher or "sage" during his earthly ministry? Second, in what way did Jesus' identity relate to that of personified Wisdom? Wisdom is treated as if it were a "lady" in Proverbs 1 and elsewhere in the Old Testament (e.g., "Wisdom cries," etc.). Later Jewish writings amplified the narrative of this female literary figure. So the question arises whether Lady Wisdom contributes to the explanation of Jesus' identity in the New Testament. It will help to clarify our study if we look at these two questions briefly here in our introduction.

We will see Jesus functioning in the role of a sage or wisdom teacher in Matthew 11, but Jesus is far more than a sage or wisdom teacher. We will also see language used of the Wisdom figure, such as her presence and role at creation, and her reflection of God's glory (John 1; Col. 1; Heb. 1). But Jesus is far more than the personification of Wisdom. We will argue in this study that it is a mistake to give too much explanatory value to the Wisdom figure in the development of the doctrine of Christ. Personified Wisdom is a way of talking about an attribute of God, and reflects some important truths about God's work in the world. But Jesus, as a distinct person, along with the Father and the Spirit, is identified as God. This divine identity of the Son is grounded in multiple Old Testament themes, as well as in the events of the life of Christ. These questions of Jesus as sage and Jesus as Wisdom personified will necessarily play a role in our study, and we will set them in their historical context in the next section of this introduction. But they are not our main focus.

The primary focal point of this study is the application of Christology to issues in the life of the New Testament church. We are investigating them in pursuit of "Christological wisdom." The church has usually studied these important texts (e.g., Phil. 2; Col. 1; Heb. 1) to develop or prove aspects of the doctrine of Christ (e.g., his preexistence, his divine nature). This is appropriate and has its place. However, we consistently find that these passages themselves are not so much developing or proving Christology as assuming it, and then applying it in various ways to the life of the church. Jesus (Matt. 11) and the gospel (1 Cor. 1) are identified in the New Testament as the unique places where God's wisdom is now revealed (Heb. 1:2; 1 Peter 1:20). The application of various elements of this revelation to problems in the life of the church is a glimpse into early Christian wisdom in practice.

Preliminary Questions

To set our study in historical perspective, it will be helpful to briefly answer four questions: What is Jewish wisdom literature? How was wisdom understood in these writings? How is wisdom different in Christ? And why are we studying these particular New Testament passages?

What Is Jewish Wisdom Literature?

We are studying Christ in relation to an ancient Jewish understanding of wisdom. This calls for a brief look at the Jewish wisdom literature found both in the Old Testament and in apocryphal books written during the period of the Second Temple.[7] The Hebrew term for wisdom (*hokmah*) in its various forms (verb, noun, adjective) occurs more than 300 times in this literature, and about three-fourths of these are in the five wisdom books discussed below.[8] The theme had become increasingly important as the New Testament period approached.

Definition of Wisdom Literature. One of the best definitions of wisdom literature is provided by James Crenshaw. He distinguishes between what this literature is *formally* and what it is *thematically*:

> *Formally*, wisdom consists of proverbial sentence or instruction, debate, intellectual reflection; *thematically*, wisdom comprises self-evident intuitions about mastering life for human betterment, groping after life's secrets with regard to innocent suffering, grappling with finitude, and quest for truth concealed in the created order and manifested in a feminine persona. When a marriage between form and content exists, there is Wisdom literature. Lacking such oneness, a given text participates in biblical wisdom to a greater or lesser extent.[9]

Some Old Testament writings, such as the psalms, by this definition are not technically wisdom literature. However, they do reflect wisdom themes. This distinction is also important for the New Testament, where we do not have wisdom literature by definition, but we do have distinct wisdom themes.

---

7. Second Temple Judaism covers the period from 516 B.C., when the Second Temple was constructed, until A.D. 70, when it was destroyed. The literature of this period, not included in the Protestant Bible, is sometimes called "intertestamental literature."

8. Cf. Roland E. Murphy, "Wisdom in the Old Testament," in *Anchor Bible Dictionary* (New York: Doubleday, 1992), 6:920.

9. James L. Crenshaw, *Old Testament Wisdom: An Introduction*, 3rd ed. (Louisville: Westminster John Knox Press, 2010), 12 (emphasis added).

Works Included in Jewish Wisdom Literature. The wisdom literature of ancient Judaism includes three Old Testament books, Job, Proverbs, and Ecclesiastes,[10] as well as two apocryphal works, Sirach (also known as the Wisdom of Jesus ben Sira or Ecclesiasticus) and Wisdom (also known as the Wisdom of Solomon). While Sirach and Wisdom of Solomon are not part of inspired Scripture, they are important literary works that provide part of the background to the New Testament.[11]

How Was Wisdom Understood in Jewish Wisdom Literature?

While this is not the place for even a brief survey of the teachings of Jewish wisdom literature, several observations will help situate our study of Christ in relation to this wisdom background.[12] There are two types of material from the wisdom literature that feed into the New Testament. First is the actual wisdom teaching. The second involves the personification of Wisdom. We will look at the personification of Wisdom below. Here we consider some of the more salient features of an Old Testament theology of wisdom.

Wisdom's voice in Israel is a form of God's self-revelation; it invites the hearer to choose between two paths; it leads to a virtuous life; it addresses the skills needed for everyday living. It also struggles with the deepest problems of life, including suffering and evil. Israel's wisdom is unique from that of the surrounding nations because it is set within the framework of God's covenantal law (Torah).[13]

10. Sometimes the Song of Solomon (Song of Songs) is included in this list.

11. A helpful resource on Jewish literature in the background of the New Testament is Richard Bauckham, *The Jewish World around the New Testament* (Grand Rapids: Baker Academic, 2010), especially chapter 14, "The Relevance of Extra-Canonical Jewish Texts to New Testament Study," 207–20. Other texts from the Apocrypha that are significant for the personification of Wisdom include Tob. 4:3–21; 12:6–13; and Bar. 3:9–4:4.

12. For two helpful works on the theology of the canonical wisdom literature, see Daniel J. Estes, *Handbook on the Wisdom Books and Psalms: Job, Psalms, Proverbs, Ecclesiastes, Song of Songs* (Grand Rapids: Baker Academic, 2010); and Daniel J. Estes, *Hear, My Son: Teaching and Learning in Proverbs 1–9* (Grand Rapids: Eerdmans, 1997).

13. This section's insights are largely adapted from Daniel Treier's excellent article "Wisdom," in *Dictionary for Theological Interpretation of the Bible*, ed. Kevin Vanhoozer (Grand Rapids: Baker Academic, 2005), 844–47.

Wisdom as Revelation. There is much in wisdom literature that is from the perspective of the wise person seeking to discern truth. Thus, it is different from prophetic material where we read, "This is what the LORD says" (e.g., Ex. 8:1). But through the human search, divine wisdom cries out; in this sense wisdom is revelatory. True wisdom for Israel is the wisdom of the Creator—their covenant God. This relationship with Yahweh is the context for all Jewish wisdom literature.

There is a tension in the literature between the accessibility of wisdom (Proverbs) and its inaccessibility (Job 28; Eccl. 7:23–29). It is accessible because of God's self-revelation, whether in creation or by his Spirit; it is inaccessible because of human finiteness and the fall.[14] God would eventually reveal his wisdom more fully in Christ. But the lesson here, from the Old Testament, is that we must remain teachable before God. As finite and fallen human beings we are dependent, through our suffering and the enigmas of life, on his gracious self-revelation.

The Two Paths. Wisdom in the Old Testament invites people to choose between two paths: that of wisdom (the way of justice) and that of folly (the way of wickedness). This is poetically captured in Psalm 1, a "wisdom" psalm. In this sense, the wisdom literature calls us to live a virtuous life, a life of godly character. But this, too, has a broader biblical context. In Genesis, Adam and Eve failed the test, choosing rather the path of folly and disobedience. Choosing the right path starts with "fearing the Lord" and then walking in obedience. This call to the path of wisdom is related to the law or Torah:

> See, I have taught you statutes and rules, as the LORD my God commanded me, that you should do them in the land that you are entering to take possession of it. Keep them and do them, for that will be your wisdom and your understanding in the sight

14. Craig Bartholomew (*Ecclesiastes* [Grand Rapids: Baker, 2009], 93) prefers to translate the word "vanity" (*hebel*) in Ecclesiastes as "enigmatic," which reflects the mystery of life apart from God's full revelation.

of the peoples, who, when they hear all these statutes, will say, "Surely this great nation is a wise and understanding people." (Deut. 4:5–6)

When Jesus came as the fulfillment of the Old Testament, including the fulfillment of its wisdom and law, he taught a parable that reflects the two paths of the wisdom literature:

> Everyone then who hears these words of mine and does them will be like a *wise* man who built his house on the rock. And the rain fell, and the floods came, and the winds blew and beat on that house, but it did not fall, because it had been founded on the rock. And everyone who hears these words of mine and does not do them will be like a *foolish* man who built his house on the sand. And the rain fell, and the floods came, and the winds blew and beat against that house, and it fell, and great was the fall of it. (Matt. 7:24–27)

Creation and Fall. Another tension found in the wisdom literature is between a good creation, in which wisdom can be discerned, and the fallen creation, in which evil and suffering exist. Job and Ecclesiastes wrestle with these problems. Both books leave the reader wanting more; this is, in part, because of their place in redemptive history. The solution to evil and suffering was still waiting for the Messiah and God's ultimate victory. When Jesus came, he would deal a death blow to evil and turn suffering upside down. But this is getting ahead of ourselves.

Wisdom and Law. We must return briefly to the question of the law in Jewish wisdom literature. In Israelite wisdom, commitment to Yahweh and his covenant is assumed (cf. Prov. 1:7; Deut. 4:5–6). The nation's wisdom literature was set in this context, including Ecclesiastes:

> The end of the matter; all has been heard. Fear God and keep his commandments, for this is the whole duty of man. For God will bring every deed into judgment, with every secret thing, whether good or evil. (Eccl. 12:13–14)

In Sirach, law and wisdom have fused even more; when wisdom speaks, it is the wisdom of Torah (Sir. 6:37; 24:22). This will have important implications for the early church, when the place of God's unique wisdom finds its fulfillment in Jesus, rather than in the law itself.

How Is Wisdom Different in Christ?

Wisdom is radically reconfigured in Christ. All preconceptions of what it means to be wise, including those of secular philosophers and religious theologians, as well as those of ordinary people, are subject to revision. There are two types of wisdom, which overlap in some ways, and yet are fundamentally different from God's wisdom in Jesus and the gospel. Since these will come up in our study, a brief look at them will be helpful.

Philosophical Wisdom. The word "philosophy" originally meant "love of wisdom." There has always been a contested relationship between philosophy and theology. At its best, philosophy has been a servant to the faith; at its worst, it has been an enemy.

Contemporary philosophers still refer to Aristotle (384–22 B.C.) for his classic treatment of wisdom. Aristotle argued that happiness came from moral virtues, and that moral virtues depended on five intellectual virtues.[15] Three of these intellectual virtues related to the contemplative life (knowledge, intuition, and wisdom); the greatest was wisdom (*sophia*). The other two intellectual virtues related to practical life (technical skill and prudence); prudence can best be translated as "practical wisdom" (*phronēsis*). Both terms for wisdom (*sophia* and *phronēsis*) are used in the New Testament with reference to God's unique wisdom in Christ.

In part, we can agree with Aristotle. Certainly moral and intellectual virtues are important, and there is much that the church needs to learn about intellectual virtues. But intellectual virtues, as understood by Aristotle or any other human philosopher, are

15. See his *Nichomachean Ethics*, especially book 6.3–7 and book 10.6–8.

not at the heart of the church's wisdom. The things that philo-sophical wisdom misses, as Augustine discovered in his journey through Greek philosophy, are Christ and the gospel.[16]

God's wisdom in Christ is not merely an idea or a theoreti-cal construction. It is grounded in historical events whereby God uniquely reveals himself. He lovingly does this so that our broken world might be set right and that we may enter into a joyful life of communion with him and with one another. While philosophical wisdom is an abstraction, God's wisdom in Christ is particular, historical, and counterintuitive to human reason. It involves the incarnation of God's Son, his death on the cross, the triumph of the resurrection, the sending of his Spirit, and the promise of a glorious re-creation of the world. It is an invitation to people everywhere to know and enjoy the triune God of Scripture in all this particularity. This is an offense to the wisdom of human philosophy.

First-Century Jewish Wisdom Speculation. There is a second kind of talk about wisdom, one that is more distinctly religious and more directly related to the gospel's historical context. In our study, a debate will surface about the relation of Jesus to personified Wisdom—or the literary figure known as "Lady Wis-dom" (also referred to as "Dame Wisdom" or "Sophia"). The Old Testament wisdom literature occasionally personifies Wisdom in this way (e.g., Prov. 1:20; 8:1). Along with a variety of other Old Testament motifs, such as God's Word and the law, this per-sonification of Wisdom is part of the conceptual background for God's revelation in Jesus. The Jewish literature mentioned above, written around the time of Christ but not included in the Bible, also contains references to Wisdom in this personified sense (e.g., Sirach, Wisdom of Solomon). We will interact with some of this background in our study.

However, some scholars have given this extrabiblical lit-erature too much explanatory value in understanding the New Testament's portrayal of Christ. They argue that the exalted

16. Carol Harrison, "Augustine, Wisdom and Classical Culture," in *Where Shall Wisdom Be Found?* ed. Stephen C. Barton (Edinburgh: T&T Clark, 1999), 137.

picture of Jesus found in the New Testament was largely the result of the early church's reflection on Lady Wisdom as a divine figure. The earliest church supposedly came to think of the human Jesus as divine because it gradually came to associate him with this first-century figure. We reject this approach for the following reasons:[17]

1. While early church fathers, after the close of the New Testament canon, sometimes identified Jesus with the Old Testament personification of Wisdom, the New Testament itself never makes this identification.[18]

2. Wisdom personified is a way of talking about an attribute of God, even in the intertestamental writings; but the New Testament teaches that Jesus is an actual person—namely, God's Son, who is included in the identity of God.

3. There are references to God's creation of Lady Wisdom in Jewish literature.[19] The New Testament portrays Jesus in his deity as eternal. It should be noted that the heretic Arius argued on the basis of the creation of Sophia that Jesus was not fully God. This was rightly rejected by the church.

4. While Lady Wisdom is described as playing a "saving" role in Israel, this never involves salvation from sin. To argue that personified Wisdom deepened the New Testament's understanding of the saving role of Jesus is to read the redemptive work of Christ into the earlier Jewish literature. The redemptive work of Christ is central to the New Testament's message about Jesus; it is absent in any substantive sense in the narratives about Lady Wisdom.[20]

---

17. Several of these reasons will be revisited and amplified during the course of this study. For a more detailed treatment of this issue, see Daniel Ebert, "Wisdom in New Testament Christology, with Special Reference to Hebrews 1:1–4" (PhD diss., Trinity Evangelical Divinity School, 1998).

18. Some argue that the identification is implied in the Gospels of Matthew and John. This is debatable; it certainly is not an explicit identification. We will also see that in 1 Corinthians 1 Jesus is identified with wisdom as the gospel and not as personified Wisdom.

19. See Prov. 8:22; Sir. 24:9.

20. A typical example of this overreading of Wisdom's salvific role can be found in Aidan O'Boyle, *Towards a Contemporary Wisdom Christology: Some Catholic Christologies in German, English and French, 1965–1995*, vol. 98 (Roma: Editrice Pontificia Università

5. Finally, the existence of a well-developed story line about a Sophia in Jewish literature is highly suspect. Scholars tend to read back into these writings elements taken from the gospel story that are foreign to what the Jewish authors in their own contexts intended. In the Jewish literature, there is no actual personal existence of Wisdom, no incarnation, no redemptive work, and no second coming.[21]

The constellation of ideas related to Lady Wisdom fails to explain the story of Jesus. At best, the background Wisdom material provided language to express truths about Christ, especially in his revelatory and creative functions. These Christological concepts were already assumed by the earliest church on other grounds. Our study rejects a Christology in which "Dame Wisdom" plays a leading role.[22] Yet there *is* a wisdom Christology, one that finds in Jesus God's fullest revelation for the church and the world.

True wisdom, rooted in the nature and life of the triune God, is revealed by Christ and the gospel. Something new and definitive is made known in Jesus; yet at the same time, this Christological wisdom is the oldest wisdom, for it is "the wisdom of God." All other conceptions, whether philosophical or religious, are judged by this wisdom.

Use of Terms. The term "wisdom" (not capitalized) will refer to the virtue of wisdom (related to other virtues such as understanding, insight, knowledge, and prudence). In the person and work of Jesus, this wisdom is revealed to have a particular shape and content; for example, it is radically self-denying and oriented

---

Gregoriana, 2003), 36, 392. The argument is usually based on Wisdom 10:1–11:1. O'Boyle writes, "The theme of unity between Sophia and God comes to significant climax in Wisdom 10 in which she is presented as Savior" (35).

21. For an example of this composite narrative of Lady Wisdom, with bibliography of other scholarly "profiles," see O'Boyle, *Towards a Contemporary Wisdom Christology*, 46–47 and n93.

22. For a helpful resource that takes a similar position, see Gordon D. Fee, *Pauline Christology: An Exegetical-Theological Study* (Peabody, MA: Hendrickson, 2008), especially Appendix A: "Christ and Personified Wisdom," 595–630, and also 102–5; 186–87; 317–25.

toward the service of others. When we speak of wisdom in this sense (i.e., in relation to Christ and the gospel), we will refer to it as "Christological wisdom."

The term "Wisdom" (capitalized) will refer to the personification or figurative portrayal of wisdom.[23] Literary personification occurs elsewhere in Scripture: for example, when justice dwells in the desert (Isa. 32:16), or when righteousness and peace kiss (Ps. 85:10). "Wisdom" may refer either to the straightforward personification of the virtue of wisdom or to the more fully developed Lady Wisdom.

One other term merits some clarification. New Testament scholars often speak of God's revelation in Christ as "eschatological." There is a growing recognition that in certain streams of first-century Judaism an eschatological wisdom was anticipated. We use the term "eschatological" in this study to refer to the dawning of the messianic age when Christ came into the world. Our life in Christ is eschatological in that we are living "between the times" of the Lord's first coming and the consummation of all things at his second coming. This Christian view of time shapes everything for the body of Christ, whose members now live defined by Christ and the wisdom found in him, even as we wait for his return.

Why Are We Studying These Particular New Testament Passages?

Understanding Christology, not just as doctrine but also as wisdom, is vital for Christian discipleship. A study of various Christological passages shows that this was the apostolic pattern. New Testament Christology was developed in applied contexts to help the church be faithful to God's revelation in his Son.

This study is necessarily selective. We have mainly chosen texts that illustrate how the apostolic doctrine of Christ was applied in the early church as wisdom for God's people.

Most of these passages share the following characteristics:

23. For consistency, we will capitalize "Wisdom" in all expressions such as "Wisdom personified," "the Wisdom figure," "Lady Wisdom," etc.

- They contain important themes about Christ, especially his identity as God's Son, as well as his roles in creation, the revelation of God, and redemption.
- They are confessional in nature; that is, they point to truths about Christ that were a part of the early church's basic beliefs about Jesus. While in one sense the entire New Testament is a confessing witness to Christ and the gospel, these texts are especially confession-like.[24]
- They all have doctrinal elements that are appropriately called creedal. Some of them appear hymnlike, or poetic, in their careful literary structure.
- All the texts are rhetorically significant: in other words, each passage plays an important role in the message of its book.
- Finally, all these texts have been discussed in New Testament scholarship with regard to Christ as wisdom.[25]

Our study will be divided into two parts. Part 1 begins with two passages from the Gospels (Matt. 11; John 1), where Jesus and the apostle John invite us to find wisdom and salvation in Christ. Part 2, the major portion of our study, examines a series of passages where God's wisdom in Christ is used richly to address particular challenges in the life of the church (1 Cor. 2; Phil. 2; Col. 1; Heb. 1).

A Warning for the Journey

A final note before we begin. Wisdom in Scripture is always set off against its nemesis—folly. Both voices call to us. This serves as a reminder that reflecting on the doctrine of Christ is never risk-free. One is always in danger of misinterpreting

24. A text that we do not treat at length, but that illustrates the confessional nature of this material, is 1 Timothy 3:16. It begins, "Great indeed, we confess, is the mystery of godliness . . ."

25. Other concentrated Christological texts could easily have been added, especially for their unusual literary structure and apparent confessional nature: e.g., Gal. 4:4–6; Eph. 2:14–16; 1 Tim. 3:16; 2 Tim. 2:11–13; Titus 3:4–7; and 1 Peter 1:17–21; 2:21–25; 3:17–22.

the biblical material or, having interpreted well, of denying the confession in life. The only way to avoid the first danger is to ask the Spirit of Christ, in keeping with the Lord's promise, to lead us into all truth (John 16:13). The only way to avoid the second is to be children of Christ's kingdom whose lives are characterized by repentance and faith. One of my earliest Bible teachers taught me that the most important question in the world was what I thought of Christ. May the Lord help us to answer that question in a way that pleases him.

Part 1

Wisdom's Invitation

Come to me,
all who labor and are heavy laden,
and I will give you rest.
Take my yoke upon you,
and learn from me,
for I am gentle and lowly in heart,
and you will find rest for your souls.
(Matt. 11:28–29)

An Invitation to Follow Jesus (Matthew 11:25-30)

At that time Jesus declared, "I thank you, Father, Lord of heaven and earth, that you have hidden these things from the wise and understanding and revealed them to little children; yes, Father, for such was your gracious will. All things have been handed over to me by my Father, and no one knows the Son except the Father, and no one knows the Father except the Son and anyone to whom the Son chooses to reveal him. Come to me, all who labor and are heavy laden, and I will give you rest. Take my yoke upon you, and learn from me, for I am gentle and lowly in heart, and you will find rest for your souls. For my yoke is easy, and my burden is light."

Introduction

What if we could slip into a gathering where Jesus was praying? Or what if we could listen to him teach? What if we saw Jesus turn to us and invite us to be his disciples? Matthew paints just such a scene for us.

The passage displays a rich and concentrated Christology. It is a Christology of action as Jesus responds to the unrepentant cities (11:1–24), prays to the Lord of heaven and earth (11:25–26), declares his unique relationship to the Father (11:27), and then invites those listening to be his disciples and enter into rest (11:28).

Before we rush in, however, we should pause, for Jesus' invitation is a dangerous one. He is offering an alternative wisdom, one that is hidden from the "wise" of this world (11:25; cf. 1 Cor. 1:18–31). It is a wisdom that, if rejected, brings awful judgment (11:22–24). It is a wisdom that requires repentance (11:20–21) and a humble, childlike faith (11:25; cf. Matt. 18:3–4; 19:14). It demands that we come radically teachable. This wisdom is also dangerous because if we accept the invitation, everything must change as we leave an old life behind and begin, through Jesus, to participate in the very life of the triune God.

As we consider this passage from the life of Jesus, a number of questions will guide us:

- What Is the Context of Matthew 11:25–30?
- What Is the Wisdom in Matthew 11:25–30?
- Is There a Wisdom Motif Elsewhere in Matthew?
- What Is the Text's Literary Background?
- How Can We Summarize Wisdom's Invitation?
- How Is This Wisdom for Us?

What Is the Context of Matthew 11:25-30?

It will help us understand this incident if we look briefly at its context and the theology of Matthew's Gospel. The chapter begins by explaining that Jesus had gone to preach in the cities (11:1). The narrative then describes how the people had rejected both John and Jesus (11:2–19). Jesus responded by teaching that these cities of Israel would experience a more severe judgment than would Tyre, Sidon, and even Sodom (11:20–24). Our section then begins with the words, "At that time Jesus declared" (11:25).

Matthew's message focuses on God's saving revelation, which centers in Jesus, the Son of God. Highlights of this theme begin with Matthew 1:23, "'Behold, the virgin shall conceive and bear a son, and they shall call his name Immanuel' (which means, God

20

with us)." Another theological high point is Peter's confession, "You are the Christ, the Son of the living God." Jesus' response to Peter uncovers the nature of divine knowledge: "flesh and blood has not revealed this to you, but my Father who is in heaven" (Matt. 16:16–17). These themes are repeated in the transfiguration scene. On that occasion, while Jesus was speaking to three of his disciples, "a bright cloud overshadowed them, and a voice from the cloud said, 'This is my beloved Son, with whom I am well pleased; listen to him'" (Matt. 17:5). The Father reveals the Son through the angelic message, through Peter, and through his own voice on the mountain.

It is in the context of this revelatory theme that Matthew 11:27 must be understood: "All things have been handed over to me by my Father, and no one knows the Son except the Father, and no one knows the Father except the Son and anyone to whom the Son chooses to reveal him." One German scholar called this text a Johannine thunderbolt, because in the midst of Matthew it sounds so much like the Gospel of John, with its high Christology and intimate relationship between the Father and the Son.[1] But the theology of the Father revealing himself in the Son, as we have seen, is thoroughly Matthean as well.

The structure of Matthew 11:25–30 can be laid out in three divisions:

1. Jesus' prayer: wisdom from the Father, vv. 25–26.
2. Jesus' claim: wisdom mediated through the Son, v. 27.
3. Jesus' invitation: wisdom offered by the Son, vv. 28–30.

As we investigate the wisdom of God in Christ, we must always keep these three lessons in mind: first, knowing God's wisdom depends on the Father's initiative; second, this wisdom is mediated through his Son; and third, some will respond in faith, while others will inevitably reject God's wisdom.

1. This epithet, "Johannine thunderbolt," can be traced back to a remark by K. A. von Hase in a work whose English translation would be *The History of Jesus* (Leipzig: Breitkopf and Hartel, 1876), 422.

What Is the Wisdom in Matthew 11:25-30?

"Wisdom" is referred to indirectly in this passage as "these things" (11:25), "all things" (11:27), and the things that can be "learned" from Jesus (11:29). Two characteristics of this wisdom are immediately clear from the passage and from the context of Matthew's Gospel: (1) the wisdom is supernaturally revealed by the Father, and (2) the wisdom concerns what the Father is doing in the Son. Whatever else can be said about this divine wisdom, it originates with the Father and focuses on the Son. What the "wise and understanding" in the normal human sense cannot grasp, the Father supernaturally "reveals" (11:25). This revelation involves the teachings of Jesus about the kingdom (11:1), his mighty works (11:2, 20), and the identity of Jesus, including his unique relationship to the Father (11:27). God the Father has "handed over" this wisdom to the Son, and the Son dispenses it to his disciples (11:27-30). Any valid interpretation of the invitation to "wisdom" in Matthew must be consistent with these basic ideas. By the end of our study we will see how comprehensive this revealed wisdom is: it is found not only in Jesus' explicit teachings, but also in his self-sacrifice on the cross and in his life as a model for his disciples, the church. We will now look at wisdom elsewhere in Matthew before considering the literary and Old Testament background for the invitation to wisdom in Matthew 11:25-30.

Is There a Wisdom Motif Elsewhere in Matthew?

The "Lady Wisdom" Question

Many scholars have suggested that Matthew reflects on the identity of Jesus in light of personified Wisdom ("Lady Wisdom"). The personification of God's attribute of wisdom is found in the Old Testament (e.g., Prov. 8) and later developed in the litera-ture between the Old and New Testaments. Such an approach to

Matthew tends to get overstated.[2] At any rate, it is insufficient to explain the wisdom wrapped up in Jesus' invitation.

Matthew is not uninterested in the question of Jesus' relation to God's wisdom. He surely is interested. The question is whether or not Matthew reflects on Jesus' identity in light of a well-developed Wisdom figure as found in the literature of the Second Temple period. While the case for identifying Jesus with "Lady Wisdom" in Matthew's Gospel is a stretch, a brief look at the arguments helps us to focus on what Matthew *is* saying about Jesus.[3]

Wisdom Justified by Her Deeds (Matthew 11:16-19)

Earlier in Matthew 11 we find these interesting words: "wisdom is justified by her deeds" (v. 19). Does Matthew here refer to Jesus as Lady Wisdom? In the context, Jesus is rebuking the people for their failure to respond to God's revelation. John came as an ascetic, and the people said he had a demon (11:18). Jesus came entering fully into social life, and the people said he was a glutton, a drunkard, and a friend of sinners (11:19). The verse ends with: "Yet [or and] wisdom is justified by her deeds." What does "wisdom" refer to here? The section begins with John the Baptist questioning Jesus' identity when John hears of "the *deeds* of the Christ" (11:2–3). The section ends with Jesus declaring that "wisdom is justified by her *deeds*." Is Matthew drawing a parallel between "the deeds of the Christ" (v. 2) and the deeds of wisdom (v. 19), identifying Jesus explicitly with wisdom or even with Sophia, the personified Wisdom figure? The distance between verse 2 and verse 19 makes an intentional verbal echo unlikely.

The phrase itself is somewhat enigmatic. What did Jesus mean when he said that "wisdom is justified by her deeds"? There

2. E.g., Celia Deutsch, "Wisdom in Matthew: Transformation of a Symbol," *Novum Testamentum* 32, 1 (1990): 13–47. See further on the Lady Wisdom question in this book's introduction.

3. See the judicious article "Wisdom," by Daniel Treier, in *Dictionary for Theological Interpretation of the Bible*, ed. Kevin Vanhoozer (Grand Rapids: Baker Academic, 2005), 844–47.

are two credible ways of interpreting this text; either one is more convincing than the "Lady Wisdom" theory. First, it might be that these are not Jesus' words, but the quoted sarcastic words of those who are rejecting Jesus. Matthew 11:19 might be punctuated this way: "The Son of Man came eating and drinking, and they say, 'Look at him! A glutton and a drunkard, a friend of tax collectors and sinners! And wisdom is justified by her deeds.'" In other words, Jesus and John are accused of violating the wisdom of the day (John's extreme asceticism and Jesus' implied drunkenness), so that neither of them is wise. This would make sense in light of Jesus' statement later, that the Father had hidden the things of Christ from the "wise and understanding" of this world (11:25). The critics completely misunderstood what God was doing in John and Jesus.

If the punctuation is left in the traditional form, then Jesus is making a final comment on the people's poor response to him and to John: "Yet wisdom is justified by her deeds." His point would simply be that both his own conduct and John's will be vindicated when understood in light of God's saving activity, that is, in light of the wisdom of the gospel. In this sense, the "deeds" of Christ and the "deeds" of wisdom *are* consonant. This may be the correct interpretation. Either way, it does not explicitly identify Jesus with the Wisdom figure. Under either interpretation, one thing is clear: the world's wisdom and what God is doing in Christ are very different understandings of wisdom.

A Wisdom Greater than Solomon's (Matthew 12:41–42)

The word "wisdom" occurs in Matthew in only two other places. Both are instructive. In chapter 12, Jesus is again rebuking the people for their unbelief and lack of repentance:

> The men of Nineveh will rise up at the judgment with this generation and condemn it, for they repented at the preaching of Jonah, and behold, something greater than Jonah is here. The queen of the South will rise up at the judgment with this generation and condemn it, for she came from the ends of the earth

24

to hear the wisdom of Solomon, and behold, something greater than Solomon is here. (Matt. 12:41–42)

It is a mistake to read this as if Jesus were identifying himself as the incarnation of Lady Wisdom. Jonah was known for his preaching; Solomon was known for his wisdom. People responded positively to them. Now something greater than either of these Old Testament figures has arrived and the people are not responding. This is Jesus' indictment. There is a parallel in Matthew 12:6 where Jesus says, "I tell you, something greater than the temple is here." The something greater, of course, is God's revelation in his Son and the promised messianic kingdom.

Matthew's wisdom is wrapped up with God's final revelation in the person and work of Jesus. We should not be unduly distracted by a supposed antecedent Wisdom figure. The focus is on judgment for lack of repentance and faith in the Messiah. If there is a typology at work, it is the typology of Jonah that is related to the resurrection (12:40) and the typology of Solomon related to the messianic king (cf. 12:23). Thus the eschatological focus: something greater is here! What this tells us is that God's wisdom has a Christological shape: the attention is fully on what God is now doing in his Son.

There is something else here that will be explicitly identified later in the New Testament as true wisdom; it relates to Solomon, Jonah, and the temple. Solomon's wisdom attracted the Gentile Queen of Sheba (1 Kings 10; 2 Chron. 9). The preaching of Jonah caused the Gentile city of Nineveh to repent (Jonah 4). The temple was intended to be "a house of prayer for all peoples" (Isa. 56:7; cf. Mark 11:17). Jesus is greater than all these because the door to the Gentiles is thrown wide open in the gospel. By the end of Matthew this will become clear, as Jesus gives the Great Commission: "Go therefore and make disciples of all nations" (28:19). Paul will forcefully identify this inclusion of the Gentiles in the purposes of God as an essential component of Christological wisdom (Rom. 16:25–27; Eph. 2:8–10; Col. 1:27–28).

25

In the first century, Gentiles were excluded from the inner precincts of the temple (Acts 21:28). But when Jesus said, "Come to me, all who labor and are heavy laden, and I will give you rest" (Matt. 11:28), his invitation was pregnant with promise for all people.

Where Did Jesus Get This Wisdom? (Matthew 13:53–58)

The noun "wisdom" also occurs when Jesus is preaching about the kingdom at Nazareth, and is met with unbelief:

> Coming to his hometown he taught them in their synagogue, so that they were astonished, and said, "Where did this man get this wisdom and these mighty works? Is not this the carpenter's son? Is not his mother called Mary? And are not his brothers James and Joseph and Simon and Judas? And are not all his sisters with us? Where then did this man get all these things?" And they took offense at him. But Jesus said to them, "A prophet is not without honor except in his hometown and in his own household." And he did not do many mighty works there, because of their unbelief. (Matt. 13:53–58)

The people in Jesus' hometown are confused about the true identity and wisdom of Jesus. They recognize him as a sage, but do not understand his true identity. They ask, perhaps sarcastically, "Where did this man get this wisdom and these mighty works?'" (13:54). Their response illustrates the prophecy of Isaiah that Jesus had referred to earlier: "You will indeed hear but never understand, and you will indeed see but never perceive" (13:14). What they cannot see and understand is what many prophets and righteous people had longed to see—the arrival of the messianic kingdom (13:17). These "things" had been hidden from the so-called "wise and understanding" (11:25).

"Where did this man get this wisdom and these mighty works?" This is the right question. Later, in writing to the Corinthians, Paul will give the answer: he connects both "wisdom" and "power" with the identity of Jesus. For those whom God has

called, both Jews and Gentiles, Jesus is "the po'
the wisdom of God" (1 Cor. 1:24). As we will s'
and power are counterintuitive in the New Te
is not found among the wise of this world, but in tʜₑ
power is not raw power, but a power manifest in weakness.

Wisdom Sends Messengers (Matthew 23:34-36)

There is another passage in Matthew where an interesting
identification of Jesus with Wisdom is possible (23:34–39). It
contains two sayings. With regard to the first saying, the point
can be seen only by comparing Matthew's account with Luke's
(Matt. 23:34–36; Luke 11:49). After a long list of "woes" to the
scribes and Pharisees, Jesus declares:

> Therefore I send you prophets and wise men and scribes, some
> of whom you will kill and crucify, and some you will flog in your
> synagogues and persecute from town to town, so that on you
> may come all the righteous blood shed on earth, from the blood
> of innocent Abel to the blood of Zechariah the son of Barachiah,
> whom you murdered between the sanctuary and the altar. Truly,
> I say to you, all these things will come upon this generation.
> (Matt. 23:34–36)

Luke identifies the speaker of these words as divine Wisdom: "Therefore also the Wisdom of God said, 'I will send them prophets'"
(Luke 11:49). Some have argued that Lady Wisdom was respon-
sible for sending the prophets in the wisdom literature. In the
figurative language of Proverbs 9, Wisdom sends out her young
women to call the simple to turn from their foolish ways (9:3–6).
In the Wisdom of Solomon, one of the apocryphal works, Wisdom
produces friends of God and prophets and causes Israel to prosper
through the prophets.[4] Was Luke thinking of Lady Wisdom when
he wrote his text? This is certainly possible, but there is nothing
else in Luke's Gospel to suggest that he had an interest in Sophia.

4. See also Wisd. 7:27; 11:1.

ᵢs may have just been his way of speaking of God's wisdom in ₍ending messengers.[5]

If Matthew was aware of Luke's wording, then he identifies Jesus with God's wisdom. But even if this is the case (and it would require Matthew to assume his readers knew Luke's wording), we should interpret it in light of what we have already seen in Matthew's Gospel. God in his wisdom hides the things of the kingdom from the unbelieving and unrepentant, from the wise and understanding of this world, but he has handed over all things to the Son. The Son, in his unique relationship with the Father, then reveals (or hides) the truth according to his will (Matt. 11:25–26). Again, this passage in Matthew reminds us of the rejection and judgment that frequently attend the invitation of wisdom and the proclamation of the gospel.[6]

Wisdom Laments (Matthew 23:37–39)

The second saying in this passage has also been read as a "lament of Lady Wisdom":[7]

> O Jerusalem, Jerusalem, the city that kills the prophets and stones those who are sent to it! How often would I have gathered your children together as a hen gathers her brood under her wings, and you would not! See, your house is left to you desolate. For I tell you, you will not see me again, until you say, "Blessed is he who comes in the name of the Lord." (Matt. 23:37–39)

If the preceding saying (Matt. 23:34–36) is not Jesus speaking as Lady Wisdom, then there is less likelihood that this saying (vv. 37–39) is to be understood in that light. While it is true that female characteristics are associated with Wisdom in the literature, it is never the figure of a hen caring for her chicks. It is the Lord in Deuteronomy 32:11 who like a mother eagle stirs

---

5. Cf. NIV translation of Luke 11:49, "God in his wisdom said, 'I will send them prophets.'"

6. See Prov. 1:22–32; 8:33, 36.

7. E.g., Deutsch, "Wisdom in Matthew," 13–47.

up her nest and hovers over her chicks and spreads her wings to catch them. In Psalm 17:8 David prays for the Lord to hide him in the shadow of his wings. This is where the children of men can find refuge (Pss. 36:7; 57:1; 63:7; 91:4). Such images may well be in the background of Jesus' prayer. The imagery suits Yahweh himself. Here, then, is another example of Matthew's high Christology, as well as the Lord's compassion for an unbelieving people. The suggestion of a reference to Sophia is unnecessary.

Summary of Jesus and Wisdom in Matthew

When these "wisdom" passages in Matthew are considered together, they paint a picture that portrays Jesus in messianic and eschatological terms. They emphasize the forward movement in redemptive history ("something greater . . . is here"): Jesus identifies himself, in a typologically suggestive way, in relation to the temple (12:6), Jonah (12:41), and Solomon (12:42). Jesus' arrival and message for all people demand a proper response. When attention is turned to the future, Jesus stands in a position of divine authority, sending authorized messengers (23:34–36). Finally, when he sorrows over Jerusalem, Jesus speaks in terms that suggest identification with God (23:37–39).

Matthew's focus is on the Son's role as the ultimate revealer of God. Matthew identifies Jesus as the promised manifestation of the Lord, whose conduct, along with that of the Lord's forerunner, will be vindicated (11:16–19). It is this Jesus, explicitly identified as God's Son and qualified to reveal the Father, who invites us to find rest in him (11:25–30) and receive his wisdom.

What Is the Text's Literary Background?

Several background texts help to shed light on Jesus and his relationship to wisdom in Matthew 11:25–30. We will first look at a text from the Apocrypha, Sirach 51, and then several Old Testament texts.

The Apocryphal Book of Sirach

Sirach, although not considered canonical by the Jews, was influential at the time of Christ. It was published in the 1611 edition of the King James Version for its historical value, but it was not considered to be Scripture. Sirach 51:23–26 reads as follows:

> Come aside to me, you untutored, and take up lodging in the house of instruction; How long will you be deprived of wisdom's food, how long will you endure such bitter thirst? I open my mouth and speak of her: gain, at no cost, wisdom for yourselves. Submit your neck to her yoke, that your mind may accept her teaching. For she is close to those who seek her, and the one who is in earnest finds her.[8]

The parallels between Matthew 11:25–30 and the description of wisdom in Sirach 51 are eye-catching. Most of them can be traced to common roots in the Old Testament. See, for example, "Come to me . . . learn from me," in such passages as Proverbs 1:24; 8:1–6; 9:5.

Perhaps the most interesting parallel in Sirach is related to Jesus' designation of the yoke as "my yoke." In Sirach 51:26 the yoke is described as belonging to wisdom: "submit your neck to *her* yoke" (cf. Sir. 6:25). What is important for our purposes is the way Sirach celebrates the law (Torah) under the guise of "wisdom."[9] Sirach 6 concludes with the words, "Reflect on the precepts of the LORD, let his commandments be your constant meditation; Then he will enlighten your mind, and the wisdom you desire he will grant" (v. 37; cf. Sir. 24:22). If there is a literary echo here in Matthew, it is one more of contrast than of identification. Jesus is not identifying himself with the wisdom of Torah as understood by much of the tradition of his day, but rather he is identifying himself as the law's fulfillment. "Take my yoke,

8. All quotes of the Apocrypha are from the *New American Bible*.

9. See James L. Crenshaw, *Old Testament Wisdom: An Introduction*, 3rd ed. (Louisville: Westminster John Knox Press, 2010), 155.

rather than that of Wisdom/Torah." Here is welcome relief, not the burden of a works-oriented rendering of Old Testament law, but rather the light yoke of gospel rest. It is the "burden" of Jesus (Matt. 11:30) and not the "burden" of the scribes and Pharisees (Matt. 23:4).[10]

There is another contrast between the invitation of Jesus and the teaching of Sirach that should be an encouragement to us. In Sirach, wisdom was largely restricted to the upper class and those who had leisure:

> The scribe's profession increases his wisdom; whoever is free from toil can become a wise man. How can he become learned who guides the plow, who thrills in wielding the goad like a lance, Who guides the ox and urges on the bullock, and whose every concern is for cattle? (Sir. 38:24–25)

Jesus, on the other hand, in the gospel invites all of us, even those who labor, to find rest and wisdom in him. This truly was a countercultural message.

Some Old Testament Background

A number of Old Testament texts shed further light on Matthew 11:29–30. Let us look at a few examples. We begin with the prophet Jeremiah:

> Thus says the LORD: "Stand by the roads, and look, and ask for the ancient paths, where the good way is; and walk in it, and find rest for your souls. But they said, 'We will not walk in it.' I set watchmen over you, saying, 'Pay attention to the sound of the trumpet!' But they said, 'We will not pay attention.'" (Jer. 6:16–19)

These words were spoken on the eve of the exile, when God was about to judge Israel. The Lord called on his people to return to

---

10. Cf. Acts 15:10, where Peter refers to the first-century interpretation of the law as "a yoke . . . that neither our fathers nor we have been able to bear."

his word so that they might find rest. Note carefully the rejection motif in Jeremiah. The people said, "We will not walk in it. . . . We will not pay attention." Surely this would have echoed in the ears of the Jews in Jesus' day. Now Jesus, as God's final and full self-disclosure, and in a similar context of rejection by God's people, was offering rest.

We find a similar and even more explicitly messianic passage in Isaiah 28:1–16:

> "Ah, . . . the drunkards of Ephraim, to whom will he teach knowledge, and to whom will he explain the message? Those who are weaned from the milk, those taken from the breast? . . . This is rest; give rest to the weary; and this is repose"; yet they would not hear. Therefore hear the word of the LORD, you scoffers . . . therefore thus says the Lord GOD, "Behold, I am the one who has laid as a foundation in Zion, a stone, a tested stone, a precious cornerstone, of a sure foundation: 'Whoever believes will not be in haste.'"

Again we have the motif of rejection, the Lord's message, children as recipients, the promise of rest for the weary, and the messianic prophecy of a sure foundation.

What these background texts indicate is that Jesus is being presented as the culmination of God's word to his people, the word that brings rest. He is the fulfillment of the former covenant and the true Torah-Wisdom (Sirach); he is the good way (Jeremiah); he is the promised, precious cornerstone (Isaiah). Exodus 33:14 reads, "My presence will go with you, and I will give you rest." In calling people to himself for rest, Jesus not only is taking the place of Wisdom and Torah, but is claiming to be the revelation of God. In Matthew's words of annunciation, Jesus is Immanuel, God with us. While the focus in our text is on the Son, in the fuller context of Matthew's good news, God is revealing himself in his Trinitarian life through the saving work of both the Son and the Spirit.[11]

11. See the helpful discussion of the role of both the Word and the Spirit in Treier, "Wisdom," 845.

How Can We Summarize Wisdom's Invitation?

We are now in a better position to summarize this glimpse into the life and teachings of Christ. In his prayer, Jesus—who alone knows the Father—teaches us about the Father, and tells us that the Father's ways are discriminating. Although he is the omnipotent Lord of heaven and earth, he chooses to reveal his wisdom to "little children." Jesus is the supreme example of true humanity, and this includes his own childhood. Although the preexistent Son of God, he was also the incarnate Son and the second Adam. In his childhood we find him in the temple, listening and asking questions (Luke 2:46), and we find him obedient and increasing in wisdom (Luke 2:52a). His childlike desire, which is a pattern for us, was toward his Father (Luke 2:52b).

It is not to the so-called "wise and understanding" of the world that God reveals his ways. The apostle Paul echoes this truth: "in the wisdom of God the world through its wisdom did not know him" (1 Cor. 1:21). The reception of God's wisdom ultimately depends on the Father's "good pleasure" (Matt. 11:26; 1 Cor. 1:21), which is oriented toward the childlike, the poor, and the weary, rather than the self-sufficient and worldly-wise. Jesus thanks the Father for this.

Jesus then makes the astounding claim that this divine wisdom is mediated through his own person. This is not a power move. Three lines of thought help to keep things in focus. First, the claim is in keeping with God's messianic work through Jesus as God's incarnate Son. This claim will eventually lead Jesus to the cross. Second, the claim is in keeping with the Savior's intimate participation in the Godhead (the mutual indwelling of Father and Son, who each "know" the other). This claim will lead Jesus to invite all to enter into the fellowship of this marvelous divine life. Finally, the Son's claim is consistent with the wisdom of God revealed in Matthew 11:25–26, particularly in its orientation toward the lowly; for Jesus, we are told, is "gentle and lowly in heart" (v. 30). This, as we will see when we get to Philippians 2, is in a counterintuitive way "godlike." So far from being a worldly "power move," Jesus' claim is one of divine self-sacrifice, which is both others-oriented and humble. Is it any wonder that the worldly-wise do not understand?

What made it particularly difficult for first-century Judaism was the shift in perspective on the law. With the gospel, the principle of interpretation shifts from the law as wisdom to Christ as wisdom (Christ being the fulfillment of the Torah). Here we see the disorientation of religious misinterpretations of Scripture, and the reconfiguration of Scripture around Christ: the former wisdom brings bondage; the latter wisdom brings rest. John will refer to this hermeneutical shift in his prologue, which we will study in the next chapter, when he says, "The law was given through Moses; grace and truth came through Jesus Christ" (John 1:17).

It may be difficult for us to imagine the impact this forward movement in God's self-revelation had in the first century with regard to the law of Moses. It would raise huge questions for the early church. For example, how does this shift affect Israel, whose basic identity markers were the stipulations of the law (e.g., circumcision, dietary laws, and holy days) and whose righteousness was tied so tightly to the law's regulations? And what about Gentiles who now become a part of God's people? How do they relate to the law? It is the apostle Paul who works out the implications of the wisdom of Christ specifically in relationship to the law.

Nothing shaped the identity of Israel, and marked her off from the surrounding Gentiles, like the Mosaic law—they understood the law as their unique wisdom. But what was God's intent in the law? In Romans 10, Paul argues that his kinsmen in Judaism had a zeal for God, but that it was not according to true "knowledge" or wisdom (Rom. 10:1). Paul helps the church at Rome to see that God's revelation in Christ was prefigured in the revelation of the law. In Romans 10:5–10, Paul interprets Deuteronomy 30, which described the provision of God's law for his people, as fulfilled in Christ. Now the wisdom of God in Christ has brought the law to its true end or culmination: righteousness by faith and eschatological salvation (Rom. 10:4). This fulfillment is found in the gospel (Rom. 10:8–10).

In Galatians 4, the apostle addressed Gentile Christians who felt pressured to submit to the law's burdensome yoke. Should these Christians succumb to a pattern of life determined more by the law than by Christ? Now that Christ had come, what should a life of wisdom look like? Paul's answer is to retell the gospel story, which comes in the form of a Christologically rich confession: God sent his preexistent Son into the world and, through the incarnation and cross, liberates people from the law's condemnation (Gal. 4:4–6). God's wisdom in Christ and the gospel not only releases believers from bondage, but also brings them into a life of adoption. God has sent the Spirit of his Son into the lives of Christians so that they, like Jesus, can know God as "Abba, Father." This life of intimacy with God, in the transforming power of the Spirit, is the new way of wisdom. It would be folly to return to the yoke of the law (Gal. 5:1, 3).

In this light we come to Jesus' grand invitation: "Come to me, all who labor and are heavy laden, and I will give you rest" (Matt. 11:28). Jesus, who as the promised messianic king and as the Son of God is in the position of ultimate rights and power, turns graciously to his audience and offers an open invitation to all the tired and burdened to come freely and enjoy rest. *This* is the wisdom of God! Here is the bondage and tutelage that will bring true rest. Here is the yoke and the burden that are easy and light, and wrapped up in the wisdom of Jesus. It is to this wisdom, then, that we are invited, that we might "learn of him."

How Is This Wisdom for Us?

Let's not miss how often God's revelation in Christ is set in a context of rejection. This has two immediate applications. First, we should not be surprised or alarmed when people, or societies at large, reject the gospel, although it should grieve us as it grieved Jesus. Second, we must examine ourselves to make sure we are among those who have "ears to hear." In a society that honors the rich, the powerful, the intellectual elite, and the famous, we must pay close attention so that we are not distracted and fail to hear God's Word. Even in our theology, we must be careful that what we think is wisdom is not actually a misunderstanding of the gospel and its implications for our lives. May we be found among the poor, the little children, and those who labor and are heavy laden.

If Jesus' invitation to wisdom resonates in our hearts, it is only because of God the Father's "gracious will" (Matt. 11:26) and the Son's sovereign favor (Matt. 11:27). Yet how generous is the Savior's invitation! Immediately after pointing out his exclusive rights as the revealer of the Father, Jesus turns to the crowd and says, "Come to me, all who labor and are heavy laden" (Matt. 11:28). The only qualification is that we not be self-sufficient and self-satisfied, but rather teachable. Jesus is not exploitive of his divine rights, as we will see in Philippians 2, but is incredibly others-oriented and generous. He is gentle and lowly in heart. If we receive his invitation to wisdom, he will teach us to be like him as well.

In this path of wisdom we receive the rest that is salvation. God's creation rest (Gen. 2:1–3; Ex. 20:11; 31:12–17) was intended as a picture of salvation rest (Heb. 4:3–4). The rest promised to the Israelites in the land of Canaan (Deut. 12:9) also pointed to the rest that comes by faith and obedience to God's Word (Ps. 95; Heb. 3:7–11; 4:8–9). The Sabbath day was another picture of God's rest. It included the rest of the seventh day, but also pointed to the rest of salvation that would come with Christ (Ex. 20:8–11; Heb. 4:9).

This promised salvation rest is found when we enter into relationship with Jesus. He offers to give us this rest when we come to him with this childlike trust. He also tells us that we will find this rest as we enter his school of wisdom and learn from him. This rest is not merely for the individual, but for "the people of God" (Heb. 4:9). As Jesus calls people to himself and to his school of discipleship, he calls a new people into being, the community that will be his body, the church. This community includes the marginalized and the lowly. It includes both the Gentiles and the Jews. How precious that this new community so graciously includes all of us!

The school of wisdom is the school of Christian discipleship. The ethical implications are huge. While Jesus' yoke is easy and his burden light, they are still a yoke and burden. The entrance into salvation comes by the work of the Spirit of Christ in our hearts, as we respond by grace through faith to the gospel call (Eph. 2:8–9). Now we enter a difficult path—one that leads to sacrificial love and the way of the cross. Here we learn "the cost of discipleship."[12] Discipleship "means to drop in behind him, to be ready to go to the cross as he did, to write oneself off in terms of any kind of importance, privilege or right, and to spend one's time only in the service of the needs of others."[13]

The Lord's greatest commandments remind us of the "learning outcomes": we are to love God, and we are to love others (Matt. 22:37–40). The core values of this school are classically summarized in the Sermon on the Mount (Matt. 5–7). Here the "wise" build their lives on obedience to the transformative words of Jesus (Matt. 7:24). According to the Great Commission, the curriculum of Christian discipleship includes learning everything that Jesus teaches (Matt. 28:20).

This invitation to wisdom requires that we be insatiable, like little children who are inquisitive, filled with wonder, and eager to learn. We must not assume that we already know the ways of Jesus, the ways of God. Neither our self-satisfied theological constructs nor our cherished ecclesiastical traditions should ever replace God's self-revelation in the Son. We must constantly ask, "What does it mean for me to follow Jesus in this situation?" and "What does it mean for us to be the church in the world today?" To properly answer these questions, we must return again and

12. This is the title of a book by Bonhoeffer that is still worth reading; see Dietrich Bonhoeffer, *The Cost of Discipleship* (New York: Simon and Schuster, 1995).

13. Ernest Best, *Disciples and Discipleship: Studies in the Gospel according to Mark* (Edinburgh: T&T Clark, 1986), 13.

again to the feet of Jesus and learn from him. Later in our study, we will see the writers of the New Testament asking and answering these very questions for the early church. These "case studies" in Christian discipleship can equip us to follow the same pattern.

Finally, we must not underestimate the invitation and the depth of this wisdom. We are being invited to participate in the divine life of the triune God. Only the Father knows the Son, and only the Son knows the Father, *and* any to whom the Son chooses to reveal the Father. The Son is inviting us into the wisdom of God: the intimate, experiential, personal knowledge shared by the Father, Son, and Spirit. This is the ultimate theological context of Jesus' invitation: "Come . . . learn from me."

In our next chapter, we will consider the invitation to God's wisdom in Christ as it is presented to us by John, the disciple Jesus loved. The introduction to his Gospel will take us even deeper into the meaning of this unique wisdom.

An Invitation to Receive the Word (John 1:1–18)

In the beginning was the Word, and the Word was with God, and the Word was God. He was in the beginning with God. All things were made through him, and without him was not any thing made that was made. In him was life, and the life was the light of men. The light shines in the darkness, and the darkness has not overcome it.

There was a man sent from God, whose name was John. He came as a witness, to bear witness about the light, that all might believe through him. He was not the light, but came to bear witness about the light.

The true light, which enlightens everyone, was coming into the world. He was in the world, and the world was made through him, yet the world did not know him. He came to his own, and his own people did not receive him. But to all who did receive him, who believed in his name, he gave the right to become children of God, who were born, not of blood nor of the will of the flesh nor of the will of man, but of God.

And the Word became flesh and dwelt among us, and we have seen his glory, glory as of the only Son from the Father, full of grace and truth. John bore witness about him, and cried out, "This was he of whom I said, 'He who comes after me ranks before me, because he was before me.'" And from his fullness we have all received, grace upon grace. For the law was given through Moses; grace and truth came through

39

Jesus Christ. No one has ever seen God; the only God, who is at the Father's side, he has made him known.

Introduction

John tells us why he wrote his Gospel: "that you may believe that Jesus is the Christ, the Son of God, and that by believing you may have life in his name" (John 20:31). The Fourth Gospel is charged with an invitation to receive God's saving wisdom in Christ, and many have come to faith reading its pages.[1] When John finished writing the main part of his book, we can imagine him composing the prologue to introduce the main themes of his Gospel (1:1–18). Much like the scene in Matthew's Gospel where Jesus invites us to enter his school of discipleship, John's prologue serves as an invitation to true wisdom. In Matthew we heard the words of Jesus; now we hear the words of his beloved disciple, reflecting deeply on the entire gospel. The invitation is the same.

As with Matthew, in John the wisdom motif needs to be interpreted with restraint and balance. Some have overread the role of the Wisdom figure for John's Gospel.[2] We will examine this tendency in more detail below. Old Testament wisdom, along with a host of other background themes, is reconfigured in the New Testament around Christ's person and work. Personified Wisdom is not a master category for the writers of the Gospels; rather, wisdom concepts and vocabulary are reinterpreted in light of God's final revelation in his Son.

In John's prologue, we are invited to participate in a Christ-centered, Trinitarian wisdom. The rejection motif is again present: some remain in darkness and will not receive this wisdom (John 1:5, 10–11; cf. 3:11; 5:43). The two paths of wisdom, as

---

1. This is not to say that John's Gospel is merely an evangelistic tract; because it is a deep proclamation and invitation to Christ's wisdom, it is also about the life of God's people, the church.

2. For example, see Sharon H. Ringe, *Wisdom's Friends: Community and Christology in the Fourth Gospel* (Louisville: Westminster John Knox Press, 1999).

in the Old Testament, are set before us; only now, we face the full and final revelation of God in Christ. For those who do respond, a far-reaching change begins to take place: people, both individually and collectively, are supernaturally transformed into God's children (1:12–13). We respond properly when we receive him and believe in his name (1:12). Those who do this are born of God (1:13), recognize God's glory in Christ (1:14), receive blessings from God's fullness (1:16), and through the wisdom revealed by Christ come to truly know God (1:18).

It has been said of John's Gospel that it is shallow enough for a gnat to wade in, but deep enough to drown an elephant.[3] The same could be said of God's wisdom in Christ, to which we are invited. In our study of John's wonderful prologue, we will consider the following:

- The Structure of John 1:1–18
- Jesus and Wisdom in John's Prologue
- Ways in Which Jesus Is More than "Wisdom"
- How Jesus Is Wisdom for Us

The Structure of John 1:1–18

To help us get at the heart of John's message, let's look at the compositional shape of his prologue. While the structural details have been greatly debated, the broad literary contours are clear. It can be laid out in an inverted fashion, where the second half mirrors the first.[4] At the center of the structure is a focus on the reception of God's saving revelation in Christ. The following outline reflects the basic flow of the passage.

3. Both the exact form and source of this saying are contested; some attribute it to the church father Augustine, but it is also said to occur in Origen. See Andreas J. Köstenberger, *Encountering John: The Gospel in Historical, Literary, and Theological Perspective*, Encountering Biblical Studies (Grand Rapids: Baker, 1999), 19.

4. This is sometimes called a chiastic pattern, after the Greek letter "chi." In such literary devices the first set of words, lines, or sections is repeated in reverse order.

A. The Word: God's Ultimate Self-Disclosure (1:1–5)
  B. John the Baptist as a Witness (1:6–8)
    C. The Incarnation (1:9–11)
      D. The Reception of the Word (1:12–13;
        cf. 20:31)
    C.' The Incarnation (1:14)
  B.' John the Baptist as a Witness (1:15)
A.' The Son: God's Ultimate Self-Disclosure (1:16–18)

In Matthew, just before inviting us to learn from him, Jesus declares his unique filial and revelatory relationship to God the Father: "All things have been handed over to me by my Father, and no one knows the Son except the Father, and no one knows the Father except the Son . . ." (Matt. 11:27). John's prologue is like a meditation on this pronouncement. No wonder the Matthew passage was called a Johannine thunderbolt! In Matthew, the Father and the Son have a mutual and exclusive knowledge. John roots this knowledge in the eternal fellowship of the Word *with* God and in the preexisting identity of the Word *as* God (1:1). This is what fully qualifies Jesus to reveal God.

In Matthew, the Son reveals the Father to whom he chooses (Matt. 11:27). In John, the apostle not only calls the Son "the Word" or God's self-expression, but also puts his revelatory work in this astonishing way: "the only God, who is at the Father's side, he has made him known" (1:18).[5] In Matthew, this revelation is sovereign: the Son reveals the Father to whom he chooses (Matt. 11:27). In John's prologue, those who participate in this transformative revelation do so by the will of God (1:13).

At the center of the prologue's structure, we find a generous invitation that echoes the Savior's words in Matthew. Again, the offer is attended by the motif of rejection. According to Matthew, the wisdom of God was hidden from "the wise and understanding," as illustrated in the cities that Jesus had just visited (Matt.

---

5. Some translations will read "the only Son," which follows an alternative reading in the Greek manuscripts. Whichever reading is followed, in context it is a reference to the divine Son. The prologue has already identified the Son as God (1:1).

11:1–24). John tells us that God's Word came "to his own, and his own people did not receive him." In Matthew's account, Jesus invites all to come and learn from him (Matt. 11:29). John states the invitation this way: "to all who did receive him, who believed in his name, he gave the right to become children of God" (1:12). Again, we see the wisdom of Jesus extending beyond the borders of Israel to the people of all nations.

We must be careful readers of Matthew and John to catch the unique ways in which they communicate their messages and to see the striking similarities as well. Both invite us to enter into the true wisdom that is found in Jesus and the gospel.

Jesus and Wisdom in John's Prologue

One of the broad types of wisdom material that scholars of Jewish and New Testament literature have identified is "higher wisdom through revelation"—wisdom that human beings cannot reach on their own.[6] John's prologue is filled with language of revelation: "word," "light," "shines," "enlightens," "witness," "glory," "truth," "made known." This revelation in John bears witness to a "higher wisdom," one that is rooted in special access to God (1:1–2, 18) and is not known by the world (1:10).

While John is using language that is similar to the vocabulary of ancient wisdom literature, we must not miss the specific theological content and focus of this "higher wisdom." John is writing that we might believe that Jesus is the Christ, the Son of God, and that by believing we may have life in his name (20:31). The "higher wisdom" must be kept in this gospel context.

The movement is from an orientation around law to one around Christ and the gospel. We already saw this implied in Matthew 11, where Jesus' yoke replaces that of the contemporary

6. John J. Collins, "Wisdom, Apocalypticism and Generic Compatibility," in *In Search of Wisdom: Essays in Memory of John G. Gammie*, ed. L. Perdue et al. (Louisville: Westminster, 1993), 168. Collins identifies four other types of wisdom material: wisdom sayings, theological wisdom (e.g., reflections on the problem of evil), nature wisdom, and mantic wisdom (e.g., wisdom to discern dreams).

understanding of Torah. John makes the underlying movement in redemptive history explicit for us: "the law was given through Moses; grace and truth came through Jesus Christ" (John 1:17). At the same time, along with this profound forward movement in redemptive history, there is also a deep continuity with the Old Testament. Jesus told the religious leaders of his day, "You search the Scriptures because you think that in them you have eternal life; and it is they that bear witness about me" (John 5:39; cf. 5:46).

The prologue uses John the Baptist's witness to ground this revelation historically in the person and work of Jesus. The goal of John's testimony is "that all might believe through him" (1:7). The reference to John's witness is repeated when we are told that he cried out, "This was he" (1:15). In the very next episode (1:19–34), John the Baptist's testimony is amplified. He tells us that Jesus is the Lamb of God who takes away the sin of the world, the one who baptizes with the Holy Spirit, and the one who is the Son of God. A faithful interpretation of the invitation to wisdom in John must operate from this historical perspective: God, the Father, was doing something in history through his Son and by the Spirit.

Ways in Which Jesus Is More than "Wisdom"

As with Matthew 11, some scholars have suggested that John's prologue, as well as his entire gospel, reflect on the identity of Jesus in light of personified Wisdom.[7] The study of the New Testament against its Old Testament and extrabiblical Jewish backgrounds is both important and precarious. In doing this work, there is a tendency for scholars to make several errors. First, assumed backgrounds may simply be mistaken.[8] Second,

7. Much of this discussion can be traced to the work of J. Rendel Harris, *The Origin of the Prologue to St. John's Gospel* (Cambridge: Cambridge University Press, 1917). See Daniel Treier, "Wisdom," in *Dictionary for Theological Interpretation of the Bible*, ed. Kevin Vanhoozer (Grand Rapids: Baker Academic, 2005), 845. Treier states that the Gospel of John arguably presents Jesus as Wisdom incarnate.

8. For example, some New Testament scholars of the last century tried to interpret New Testament Christology against a purported gnostic redeemer myth. This is now widely

legitimate background language or conceptions may be overinterpreted, especially under the influence of the New Testament itself. In other words, similar material from a variety of background sources is reconstructed around a narrative component provided by the New Testament, and then read as explaining the New Testament itself. Finally, scholars sometimes view the complexity of the New Testament message reductionistically, in light of the argued background motif: that is, a single background conception may be given too much explanatory value. These problems apply to the way some interpreters treat the theme of wisdom. There *is* a wisdom background to the New Testament's understanding of Christ, but it must be interpreted with care and balance.

Upon careful examination, many of the supposed parallels between Jesus in John and Wisdom in the preceding literature break down. Furthermore, a complete story of "Lady Wisdom" is not found in any of the background material. Scholars tend to compose a Wisdom narrative by a selective and somewhat forced reading of a variety of rather disparate Jewish texts. A case can be made that at least parts of this account are read back into the Jewish material from the perspective of the New Testament gospel narrative. John's portrayal of Jesus in his prologue moves beyond anything ever taught about personified Wisdom in the Old Testament or in extrabiblical Jewish literature. A brief examination of three themes in John 1:1-18 will help us to focus on what John *is* saying about Jesus.

The Son's Preexistence (John 1:1-5)

As the Son of God. Three features in John's presentation of the Son's preexistence are theologically important and distinguish Jesus from all other background figures, including Wisdom. First, the Word was not created: he simply "was" (John 1:1). In Sirach 24:9, the Jewish apocryphal work we looked at in the last chapter, Wisdom says, "Before all ages, in the beginning, he created me,

---

recognized to be mistaken, since a full-fledged gnostic redeemer figure developed only after the time of the New Testament.

and through all ages I shall not cease to be."[9] When John speaks of God's Son, he is not speaking of the mere personification of the divine creative speech; he is referring to a unique person who existed before the world began (John 17:5; 1 John 1:2; 2:13). Wisdom is described as created; the Word is not. This is a vital theological difference. Jesus said, "Truly, truly, I say to you, before Abraham was, I am" (John 8:58). The uncreated second person of the Godhead is an essential component of biblical Christology. He is the one who is able to save us to the uttermost (Heb. 7:29).

Second, the Word was in personal communion with the Father: "and the Word was *with* God" (John 1:1). The preposition "with" in this context, repeated in John 1:2, suggests a personal relationship. This is confirmed by the structural parallel in John 1:18, where this intimate relationship is described as the Son being "at the Father's side." Jesus explains this later in John when he prays, "Father, glorify me in your own presence with the glory that I had with you before the world existed" (John 17:5). It is true that Wisdom at creation describes herself as "daily his delight, rejoicing before him always" (Prov. 8:30). In one sense, this does provide a typological representation of the joyful fellowship experienced within the Godhead: the Father and the Son, along with the Holy Spirit, enjoy one another in intimate communion. It was the return to this joy shared with the Father that Jesus envisioned even as he endured the cross (Heb. 12:2). In the gospel, the Holy Spirit will reproduce this joy as a fruit in the life of Christ's disciples (Gal. 5:22). The picture of Wisdom being God's delight and rejoicing before him is suggestive of this relationship, but the boundaries of previous Jewish Wisdom speculation are clearly crossed here.

John is not speaking about the personification of an attribute of God, nor about a created Wisdom figure, but about the eternal Son of God in unique fellowship with the Father. This special rela-

9. All quotations of the Apocrypha in this chapter are from the *New American Bible*. Cf. Prov. 8:22. There is a debate as to whether the Hebrew word in Proverbs 8:22 should be translated as "created" or "acquired." The Septuagint translates it as "create," and Sirach uses the Greek word for "create." See Ringe, *Wisdom's Friends*, 36 and n19.

tionship that the Son has with the Father is the ultimate grounds for our entrance into intimate fellowship with God. It is why Jesus said to doubting Thomas, "I am the way, and the truth, and the life. No one comes to the Father except through me" (John 14:6). Jesus invited us to enter into perfect communion with the Father, one that he enjoys as God's Son.

The third feature of Jesus' preexistence is the most astounding. What is now predicated of the Word would be unthinkable with regard to Wisdom. Not only is the pre-creation existence of the Word, and the unique relationship of the Word to the Father, significantly beyond what is stated of Lady Wisdom, but the Word actually *was* God! This expression boldly announces the deity of the Son. What is critical in this emphasis on the full deity of Christ is the focus on the Son's revelatory function as "the Word."

Like the ancient literary figure of Wisdom, Jesus reveals God and his ways. But in his full identity as the divine Son, and consequently in his ability to reveal God, Jesus far surpasses all other religious figures. The Word is vastly superior to any preceding revelation. This personal revelation, of one who is included in the identity of God, means that there can be no future revelation superior to God's Son and the gospel. Is it any wonder that Peter asked Jesus, "Lord, to whom shall we go? You have the words of eternal life" (John 6:68).

As the Agent of Creation. The Son's role in creation is another key component in New Testament Christology.[10] John declares, "All things were made through him, and without him was not any thing made that was made" (John 1:3).

Readers of the Bible have often noticed the similarity between the beginning of John's prologue ("In the beginning was the Word") and Genesis 1:1 ("In the beginning God created"). In the Old Testament, both Proverbs 3 and Proverbs 8 speak of Wisdom's role at creation. In Proverbs 3 we are told, "The LORD by wisdom founded the earth; by understanding he established the heavens" (3:19). In Proverbs 8, personified Wisdom speaks: "When he established

10. See the important recent study by Sean H. McDonough, *Christ as Creator: Origins of a New Testament Doctrine* (New York: Oxford University Press, 2009).

the heavens, I was there . . . When he marked out the foundations of the earth, then I was beside him, like a master workman" (8:27–30). There is an interesting rabbinic gloss on Genesis 1:1 that reads, "In the beginning God *by wisdom* created the heavens and earth."[11] In light of this background material, it is not surprising that readers of John's prologue would associate the Son's creative role with this antecedent creative function of Wisdom. Wisdom's role at creation is perhaps the strongest argument for interpreting Christology in light of Wisdom. But we must remind ourselves of several factors that help us to interpret John faithfully.

First, as we have seen, a one-to-one correspondence between the Son and personified Wisdom breaks down. Wisdom is described as created; the Son is eternally preexistent. Second, Wisdom is only one metaphor under which God's creative work is described in the background material.[12] This reminds us that the New Testament identifies Christ, God's Son, as the divine agent of creation, and the various antecedent expressions are but helpful conceptual tools to describe his role.

Finally, we need to ask: What is John doing when he states that the Son is the one through whom all things come into existence? What is his rhetorical purpose? While it is appropriate to see God's revelation in his Son functioning as wisdom, it is also important to note that John never uses either the word "wisdom" or the word "wise" in his prologue or Gospel. Clearly, John's intention is not to make an explicit identification between the Word and personified Wisdom—to do this would have fallen far short of his theological goal. What then is John doing when he links the Word with the work of creation?

His primary purpose is directly related to the function of his Gospel. John wants to magnify for us the revelatory power of Jesus Christ. Here is one who is the very self-expression (the

11. Creation is also connected with the Torah or Law in rabbinic glosses on Genesis 1:1. See Craig Evans, *Word and Glory: On the Exegetical and Theological Background of John's Prologue*, Journal for the Study of the New Testament Supplement Series 89 (Sheffield, UK: JSOT Press, 1993), 114–34.

12. In Jewish intertestamental literature, creation is also accomplished, for example, by God's Spirit, God's Son, God's power, God's Word, and God's law.

Word) of God, who was with God, and who was God. His revelatory power is so great that the whole created order came into being by him. His revelatory power is so great that it brings life and light. This light shines in the darkness, even as God's creative Word spoke light into the primordial darkness, and the darkness cannot resist it. Christ had played an active role in God's revelation in the Old Testament but also through general revelation: God's self-revelation through history, creation, and human conscience. Now this light is shining on all people through the gospel. This is the light that is offered to us. It is one thing to argue for the deity of Christ; it is another thing to know God experientially through the wisdom to which the supremely qualified Jesus invites us.[13]

At best, personified Wisdom can provide only a partial explanation of John's language and categories. The new component must not be underestimated. "The 'absolute' description of the Word that was with God and that was God (1:1) is explained at the deepest level, by the absoluteness of the historic self-disclosure of Jesus as the Christ, the Son of God."[14] This is the wisdom that can save us and teach us how to live.

The Son's Incarnation (John 1:6–14a)

The prologue speaks clearly of the Son's incarnation. John tells us that "the true light . . . was coming into the world" (1:9) and that "he came to his own" (1:11). The structural parallel develops the theme, "and the Word became flesh and dwelt among us" (1:14). The identity of this light and this Word is clear. He is "the only Son from the Father" (1:14), and again he is "the only God, who is at the Father's side" (1:18). Lest we miss it, John tells us exactly whom he is talking about—Jesus Christ (1:17). This last point is essential, especially when looking at various possible backgrounds to John's prologue. John's purpose, as he has told us, is "that you may believe that Jesus is the Christ, the Son

13. See 1 John 1:5–10, where John makes this invitation to the light.
14. Herman Ridderbos, *The Gospel according to John: A Theological Commentary*, trans. John Vriend (Grand Rapids: Eerdmans, 1997 [original 1987]), 5.

of God" (John 20:31). The subject of John's Gospel is Jesus, and everything he says in the prologue is about this same person. It is Jesus, God's Son, who has become incarnate.

This is verified when we look at the Lord's own claims in the narrative. In his night conversation with Nicodemus, Jesus declared, "No one has ascended into heaven except he who descended from heaven, the Son of Man" (John 3:13). In John 6:38 Jesus says, "I have come down from heaven, not to do my own will but the will of him who sent me." This offended those from his hometown, who responded, "Is not this Jesus, the son of Joseph, whose father and mother we know? How does he now say, 'I have come down from heaven'?" (John 6:42). All this must be kept in mind as we consider the purported wisdom background to the incarnation.

Some have appealed to the journey of personified Wisdom to account for John's motif of Jesus descending from heaven and returning to heaven.[15] But it is doubtful that such a Wisdom narrative conceptually influenced John on the incarnation. In the broader religious milieu of the New Testament, the category of a descending/ascending figure was arguably widespread.[16] However, just because the motif occurs in one religious context does not give it explanatory value for a totally different context. Furthermore, it is highly unlikely that there was a well-developed descending/ascending Wisdom story in Jewish literature before the time of the New Testament. The literature portrays Wisdom as coming from heaven, but this may simply be a way of speaking about God's revelation in general, although at times in a way that is personified under the figure of Wisdom.[17] This is hardly parallel with an actual incarnation. Furthermore, the few references to the "ascent" of Wisdom are not clearly ascents, but the withdrawal of understanding from God's people.[18] In none of this literature is

15. D. Burkett, *The Son of Man in the Gospel of John*, Journal for the Study of the New Testament Supplement Series 56 (Sheffield, UK: JSOT Press, 1991), 30–33.

16. C. H. Talbert, "The Myth of a Descending-Ascending Redeemer in Mediterranean Antiquity," in *New Testament Studies* 22 (July 1976): 418–43.

17. For the more important apocryphal texts, see Wisd. 9:9–10, 17; Sir. 24:3–12; Bar. 3:28–29.

18. See 2 Esd. 5:9–10; 2 Bar. 48:36.

there a complete narrative of a personified Wisdom descending from heaven and then ascending to heaven. The only Jewish text that combines these two ideas is 1 Enoch 42:1–2, which reads:

> Wisdom found no place where she might dwell;
> Then a dwelling-place was assigned her in the heavens.
> Wisdom went forth to make her dwelling among the children
>   of men,
> And found no dwelling-place:
> Wisdom returned to her place,
> And took her seat among the angels.[19]

The dating of this work is disputed, but in any case this rather odd document hardly constitutes a Wisdom descent/ascent pattern for Second Temple Jewish literature.[20] To suggest that John had this type of Jewish Wisdom story in mind is not convincing. There are no substantive parallels in the Jewish literature for the incarnation. In John's prologue, we are moving well beyond anything ever said of Wisdom.

John is speaking of the incarnation of God's Son, whom the readers would recognize from the Fourth Gospel and their exposure to the Christian movement as Jesus, the Christ. In Matthew's language, we are dealing with Immanuel, "God with us" (Matt. 1:23). John speaks of him under the title of "the Word" because this was an appropriate expression to stress the supremacy and finality of God's revelation in Christ. This encompasses and brings God's revealed wisdom to its culmination. This wisdom finds its new orientation in the Gospel narrative, and it is to this wisdom that we are invited.

Here are the questions we should be asking ourselves: What exactly is this wisdom like? How can we participate in it? John continues by telling us what the first disciples saw: it was the

19. R. H. Charles, ed., *The Apocrypha and Pseudepigrapha of the Old Testament in English*, vol. 2 (Oxford: Clarendon Press, 1913), 213.
20. This section of 1 Enoch is known as the *Book of Parables of Enoch* (1 Enoch 37–71), and is also called the *Similitudes of Enoch*. Some think it is post-Christian, while others argue for an earlier date.

Son's incarnate glory. This will lead us closer to the essence of God's wisdom in Christ.

The Son's Glory (John 1:14b–18)

The motif of "glory" in John's Gospel is worthy of careful attention. Here in the prologue we notice three things that help us see the nature of the wisdom that John is announcing. First, the glory is wrapped up with what the incarnate Son reveals about the Father ("as of the only Son from the Father" [1:14]). Second, the glory is described as marked by "grace and truth" (1:14, 16–17). And finally, the glory is tied to both John the Baptist's testimony (1:15) and the apostolic witness ("the Word became flesh and dwelt among *us*, and *we* have seen his glory" [1:14]). There is perhaps no better commentary on this than what John wrote in his First Epistle:

> That which was from the beginning, which we have heard, which we have seen with our eyes, which we looked upon and have touched with our hands, concerning the word of life—the life was made manifest, and we have seen it, and testify to it and proclaim to you the eternal life, which was with the Father and was made manifest to us—that which we have seen and heard we proclaim also to you, so that you too may have fellowship with us; and indeed our fellowship is with the Father and with his Son Jesus Christ. (1 John 1:1–3)

Here then is the invitation to wisdom. It is an invitation through the gospel to enter into fellowship with the triune God and to participate in his divine life and glory.

The reference to glory (1:14) is not to the Son's exaltation, but to the divine self-revelation manifested in Christ's life and ministry. The Wisdom pattern of preexistence (with God), earthly existence (descent), and then existence in heaven (ascent/glory) is inadequate here.[21] This calls into further ques-

---

21. This pattern has been argued, for example, by Ben Witherington III, *John's Wisdom: A Commentary on the Fourth Gospel* (Louisville: Westminster John Knox Press, 1995), 48–49.

tion the usefulness of the so-called Wisdom myth or narrative for explaining John's Christology, especially in the prologue. Our attention should be directed to Jesus. What does he do for us on the cross, and what do his life and death teach us about how we ought to live?

How Jesus Is Wisdom for Us

A Summary of the Wisdom Invitation

In John's introduction, we have three of the major themes of Christ as the wisdom of God: revelation, creation, and redemption. These themes will remain important throughout our study.

When we consider the Son's preexistence, the nature of his role in creation, his incarnation, and his glory, it is clear that while there are parallels, this revelation far exceeds that of any preceding revelatory figure. It is a wisdom wrapped up with the true subject of the prologue, Jesus "the Messiah" (John 1:17).

Wisdom and the Person and Work of Jesus

The preexistent one's incarnation is related to the forward movement in redemptive history, and the movement from a focus on the law of Moses to a focus on "grace and truth" (John 1:17). Thus, it is a wisdom tied up with the life and ministry of the earthly Jesus in whom this glory is seen. The double reference to John the Baptist's witness (John 1:6-8, 15), so crucial to the message of the prologue and immediately tied to the narrative that follows (John 1:19-23), binds John's high Christology to the earthly Jesus. Wisdom, originating in the eternal Godhead, is now to be found in the person, life, teaching, and work of Jesus. No one has ever seen God, but Jesus, who is supremely qualified as God's own Son, teaches us about him (John 1:18). It is to this teacher and to this teaching that we are invited. This is the school of wisdom for us.

Wisdom and the Church

We must not miss the communal nature of this invitation. The Word had come to his own people, but they rejected him. However, those who receive Christ have the right to be called "children of God" (John 1:12), and together they form the new community of the church. It was the apostolic circle that saw the Son's glory (John 1:14) and received grace and blessing from him (John 1:16). They have passed on to us this testimony and invitation. As John wrote later to the early church, "that which we have seen and heard we proclaim also to you, so that you too may have fellowship with us; and indeed our fellowship is with the Father and with his Son Jesus Christ" (1 John 1:3). The invitation to the wisdom of God in Christ is an invitation to participate in the life of God's people, the church. It is also an invitation to live as a reflection of the Lord's glory. Paul teaches that it is through the church that the manifold wisdom of God is made known even in heavenly places (Eph. 3:10).

Wisdom and Scripture

Notice what has been happening here with Scripture. The historical Jesus gave his invitation to his disciples while ministering in Israel. The Gospel writer, who was part of the earliest community, recorded the invitation in what we know as the Gospel of Matthew (Matt. 11:25–30). Now John, in his Gospel, has likewise written an account, in which he reflects on the life and teachings of Jesus. The Lord had promised that he and the Father would send the Holy Spirit to his people, and that the Spirit would lead the disciples into all truth (John 16:13). This was happening even as the New Testament canon was taking shape. The invitation to wisdom is an invitation to participate in the life of the church, but also to learn from the written Word, which the triune God has entrusted to his people. Paul tells Timothy that the Scriptures are able to make one "wise" in a way that leads to salvation (2 Tim. 3:15). This was coming to include the New Testament documents. As we study Scripture in the church, under the guidance of the Spirit, and as we live out its message together, we participate in the wisdom of God revealed in Jesus Christ.[22]

Let us not miss the grandeur and wonder of this invitation to wisdom. We are being invited individually and collectively into intimate fellowship with the triune God. Matthew taught us that only the Father knows the Son, and only the Son knows the Father (*and* any to whom the Son chooses to reveal the Father). John has taught us that no one has ever seen God, but that Jesus reveals him to us. This then is the invitation—to truly know God and, together as his children, to become like him through participation in the person and work of his unique Son, Jesus Christ.

In the New Testament texts that we will study in the following chapters, we will see how the earliest church was being instructed, often in very practical ways, to faithfully live out this wisdom.

22. For a helpful recent book on the doctrine of Scripture, see Timothy Ward, *Words of Life: Scripture as the Living and Active Word of God* (Downers Grove, IL: IVP Academic, 2009), especially chapter 5, "The Bible and the Christian Life: The Doctrine of Scripture Applied."

Part 2

Wisdom and the Cross

We preach Christ crucified,
a stumbling block to Jews and folly to Gentiles,
but to those who are called, both Jews and Greeks,
Christ the power of God and the wisdom of God.
For the foolishness of God is wiser than men,
and the weakness of God is stronger than men. . . .
He is the source of your life in Christ Jesus,
whom God made our wisdom and our righteousness
and sanctification and redemption.
(1 Cor. 1:23–25, 30)

Wisdom and the Crucified Christ (1 Corinthians 1:18-24, 30-31; 8:6)

For the word of the cross is folly to those who are perishing, but to us who are being saved it is the power of God. For it is written, "I will destroy the wisdom of the wise, and the discernment of the discerning I will thwart." Where is the one who is wise? Where is the scribe? Where is the debater of this age? Has not God made foolish the wisdom of the world? For since, in the wisdom of God, the world did not know God through wisdom, it pleased God through the folly of what we preach to save those who believe. For Jews demand signs and Greeks seek wisdom, but we preach Christ crucified, a stumbling block to Jews and folly to Gentiles, but to those who are called, both Jews and Greeks, Christ the power of God and the wisdom of God. . . . He is the source of your life in Christ Jesus, whom God made our wisdom and our righteousness and sanctification and redemption. Therefore, as it is written, "Let the one who boasts, boast in the Lord." . . . For us there is one God, the Father, from whom are all things and for whom we exist, and one Lord, Jesus Christ, through whom are all things and through whom we exist.

Introduction

One of the most devastating experiences Christians can have is to be involved in a church split. It can discourage the most mature believer, tear families apart, and harm the church's testimony. Typically, each side of a squabble is convinced it is right. Arguments pile up, and a proud party spirit spreads like cancer. Soon the inevitable blowup comes, and worldly wisdom wins the day.

One of the major problems that Paul faced at Corinth was a divisive spirit characterized by claims to wisdom (1 Cor. 1:10–11). It is in response to this problem that the apostle explicitly identifies Christ and the wisdom of God (1 Cor. 1:24, 30). Grasping what Paul is teaching here can help us understand more clearly God's wisdom in Christ. It can also serve as a remedy for the continuing problem of church divisions, especially those based on a misplaced confidence in human wisdom.

We must clarify what Paul is and is not saying about Christ and wisdom. Paul uses the words "wisdom" and "wise" frequently in 1 Corinthians 1–3. Because of this, some have suggested that there was a presence of Jewish wisdom speculation at Corinth, and that perhaps Paul is responding to this by identifying Christ against the backdrop of a personified Wisdom figure. But as we will see, this is a misreading of the situation and Paul's teaching. We will begin by exploring what the problem might have been at Corinth with regard to wisdom. Then we will look at Paul's language and teaching in 1 Corinthians 1:24, 30. Finally, we will look at 1 Corinthians 8:6, one of Paul's most important statements about Christ. Here is a road map for this chapter:

- The "Wisdom" Problem at Corinth
- Paul's Wisdom Language in 1 Corinthians
- Paul's Positive Teaching on Wisdom
- 1 Corinthians 8:6 as an Example of Wisdom Applied
- Wisdom for Us

The "Wisdom" Problem at Corinth

Paul is treating wisdom, and Christ as God's wisdom, as a response to the reported divisions in the Corinthian church. What was causing these divisions? What was the nature of the problem that Paul was confronting? Various theories have been proposed. Was there a group at Corinth influenced by the kind of thinking that was such a problem in Galatia—a legalistic party pressuring Gentiles to comply with the food laws and other ceremonial requirements of Judaism? Paul mentions some at Corinth who were claiming, "I follow Cephas [Peter]" (1 Cor. 1:12). While there might have been some legalism at Corinth, it does not seem to be a primary problem. This would be to read Galatians into 1 Corinthians, and there is nothing to indicate here an ongoing tension between Peter and Paul, or that the issue is related to an imposition of Jewish ceremonial law on Gentiles. In fact, it is not the Jews who are celebrating wisdom here, but the "Greeks" (1 Cor. 1:22).

Others have suggested that perhaps Paul was responding to a myth at Corinth that celebrated wisdom on the basis of either a Greek mythological figure or a Jewish Wisdom figure. Paul would then be responding to such a myth by arguing that Christ is truly the wisdom of God, and not some other figure. But such theories appear to overinterpret the wisdom language and misread what Paul is saying. A closer look at the text suggests that the problem is not a contrary teacher or theology, but a pastoral issue. Paul is responding to a party spirit that could well be emanating from leaders of some of the house churches in Corinth. Paul's concern is not primarily the content of their teachings. There was likely a mix of theological and practical problems behind the controversy reflected in 1 Corinthians 1–3. However, the basic issue appears to be inappropriate competitiveness based on confidence in human wisdom. Paul's stated aim is not to deal with heresy, but to remedy the problems of discord and a partisan spirit. A closer look at Paul's wisdom language helps to clarify this.

61

Paul's Wisdom Language in 1 Corinthians

The Greek word for "wisdom" occurs infrequently in the New Testament. More than half the occurrences (28) are in Paul's epistles. Most (16) are in the context of the problem at Corinth. A similar pattern occurs for the word "wise." Paul uses "wisdom" and "wise" a total of 44 times, and over half of these are in 1 Corinthians 1–3. Furthermore, most of the uses of these words in 1 Corinthians 1–3 are in a negative or pejorative sense. Words and statistics are tricky things, and one needs to draw conclusions carefully. At least three things are clear. First, relative to other important theological terms used by Paul, "wisdom"/"wise" is not used often. Second, a preponderance of Paul's uses is here in 1 Corinthians 1–3, and most of these are in a negative sense. Finally, however, Paul does use the wisdom language in a positive sense, and when he does so, it is with reference to Christ and the gospel.

Paul uses the vocabulary of "wisdom"/"wise" with at least three senses in 1 Corinthians 1–3. He uses it in a negative sense of the world's thinking apart from the gospel, although he does not identify any specific doctrines (1 Cor. 1:20–21, 25; 2:13). He uses it negatively of verbal skill, eloquence, or rhetoric (1 Cor. 1:17, 20; 2:1, 4–5, 13; see also 1 Cor. 3:18–20). These two uses are related and suggest that the background against which Paul's discussion of divine wisdom should be read is the self-confident thinking of the Corinthians, who took pride in rhetorical ability.[1] Certain house-church leaders may have been taking advantage of this attitude.

Finally, Paul uses the "wisdom" vocabulary in a positive sense when speaking of God's wisdom (1 Cor. 1:21, 24, 30; 2:6–7). Clearly, Paul rejects the content of the Corinthians' worldly wisdom. Whatever that wisdom might be, the apostle is not interested either in it or in its eloquent ways. But there is a supernaturally revealed wisdom that Paul celebrates and

1. This tendency at Corinth is also evident in Paul's somewhat sarcastic comments in 1 Corinthians 6:5 and 2 Corinthians 11:19.

holds up for the Corinthians to embrace: God's wisdom in Christ and the gospel.[2]

Paul's Positive Teaching on Wisdom

The Colossian and Ephesian Parallels

A brief look at the use of the wisdom terms in Ephesians and Colossians confirms that Paul does think of wisdom in a positive light with regard to the gospel.[3] While the apostle does warn believers of mere human wisdom or "an appearance of wisdom" (Col. 2:23), he also emphatically celebrates God's wisdom in Christ.

In both epistles Paul teaches that this wisdom is absolutely dependent on divine revelation. God has "lavished upon us" the saving grace of the gospel "in all wisdom and insight" (Eph. 1:8). It is God who gives believers "a spirit of wisdom and of revelation in the knowledge of [Christ]" (Eph. 1:17). In Colossians, Paul prays that God will fill the saints "with the knowledge of his will in all spiritual wisdom and understanding" (1:9).

For Paul, this wisdom is uniquely located in Christ. He proclaims Christ, "warning everyone and teaching everyone with all wisdom" to present everyone "mature in Christ" (Col. 1:28). It is in Christ that "are hidden all the treasures of wisdom and knowledge" (Col. 2:3).

2. Gordon Fee, *Pauline Christology: An Exegetical-Theological Study* (Peabody, MA: Hendrickson, 2008), 103, seems to overstate the case when he writes, "It is especially doubtful whether 'wisdom' is a truly Pauline word at all." This is understandable. Fee's concern is to refute any explicit or implicit association in Paul's mind between Christ and the Jewish Wisdom figure. While this is a needed corrective, one can still leave place for Paul to think of Christ explicitly in terms of divine wisdom, although not in terms of a preexisting Jewish figure or myth. Fee categorizes such positive uses of wisdom as references to an "attribute" of God.

3. See also Romans, where Paul divides people into the wise and foolish (1:14), identifies false claims to wisdom as leading to folly (1:22), warns believers against their own human wisdom (11:25; 12:16), encourages wisdom related to what is good in the context of Christian obedience (16:19), and celebrates God's ineffable wisdom as revealed in the gospel (11:33; cf. 16:27).

In Ephesians, Paul teaches that this "manifold wisdom of God" is made known "through the church" even in heavenly places (Eph. 3:10). Because of this role of the church in the mission of God, it is important for God's wisdom in Christ to shape the lives of believers, both in communal life and in their witness to the world. We are to let the Word of Christ dwell in us richly, "teaching and admonishing one another in all wisdom" (Col. 3:16). Toward outsiders we are to "walk in wisdom" (Col. 4:5) and to think deeply about how we live, as people who are truly "wise" (Eph. 5:15). This is not a generic philosophical wisdom that transforms our lives, but God's unique and often counterintuitive wisdom found in Christ and the gospel. Colossians and Ephesians present Paul's most extended teaching on God's wisdom.[4] This summary of the apostle's teaching will help to keep Paul's theology in focus as we examine his treatment of Christ as wisdom in 1 Corinthians 1.

Paul's Explicit Teaching in 1 Corinthians

In 1 Corinthians 1:24 and 30 Paul does what is not done elsewhere in the New Testament: he calls Christ "wisdom." For the elect, Christ is "the wisdom of God" (1:24), and again for those who are in him, God has made Christ "our wisdom" (1:30). It has been common for scholars to suggest that Paul is ascribing to Christ the salvation that the Jewish wisdom tradition had attributed to Wisdom.[5] Some even think the relation between Christ and God's wisdom here suggests that in Paul's mind there was, at least to a degree, an identification of Christ with the Jewish figure of Wisdom. This, however, is the direction of neither New Testament teaching nor Paul's thought.

4. We will take a closer look at Colossians 1:15–20 in the next chapter. Ephesians merits a separate chapter, especially for its focus on wisdom and the church; in this book we can only point out its importance and make reference to its parallel themes along the way.

5. See F. F. Bruce, *1 & 2 Corinthians*, New Century Bible Commentary (London: Marshall, Morgan, and Scott, 1971), 35–36. More recently, see David G. Horrell, *An Introduction to the Study of Paul* (London: T&T Clark, 2006). Horrell argues that Paul has "adopted and adapted these various Jewish traditions for speaking about God's attributes and agents, and applied them to Christ" (66).

When Paul says that Christ is "the power of God and the wisdom of God" (1 Cor. 1:24), this is not a statement of identity between two persons or figures. Such an identification can be made only if the words "Christ . . . the wisdom of God" are artificially extracted from the context and read against a different background and teaching. For Paul, the location of wisdom is explicitly in the divine plan of revelation and salvation that climaxes in the gospel and centers on Christ. There is no hint of an allusion to, or a dependence on, a Jewish Wisdom figure. Christ sent the apostle "to preach the gospel . . . the cross of Christ" or the "word of the cross" (1 Cor. 1:17–18). It pleased God in his wisdom to save those who believe through the preaching of the gospel (1 Cor. 1:21). First Corinthians 1:18–25 should be read as one cohesive paragraph; it begins and ends with the same point: the gospel is God's counterintuitive wisdom and power (cf. Rom. 1:16).

The focus of wisdom in the New Testament is the cross. Christ's crucifixion has a twofold characteristic: it is both the wisdom of God and the power of God. This couplet of wisdom and power occurs in Mark 6:2 (cf. Matt. 13:54), where the crowd asks, "Where did this man get these things? What is the wisdom given to him? How are such mighty works done by his hands?"[6] Mark's Gospel is identifying Jesus through this narrative as the Son of God and the Messiah. Paul, at a later point in redemptive history, identifies Christ for the church as "the power of God and the wisdom of God" (1 Cor. 1:24). From Paul's vantage point, now that Christ has died and risen from the dead, this identification is wrapped up not merely with Jesus' public works of ministry, but most essentially with his crucifixion.

The "word of the cross" is to the unbeliever foolishness, but to those being saved it is "the power of God" (1 Cor. 1:18). Paul preaches "Christ crucified," to the unbeliever a stumbling block and foolishness, but to the elect the "power of God" and "the wisdom of God" (1 Cor. 1:23–24). The couplet is significant, showing

6. See Job 12:13–16, where the couplet also occurs.

65

that we are not dealing with a one-to-one correspondence between Christ as a person and the figure of Wisdom. No one would argue that Christ is the personified power of God on the basis of this statement. Such identification between Christ and the Wisdom figure, though often repeated, ought to be laid to rest.[7]

This interpretation is confirmed by 1 Corinthians 2:6–8, where Paul says that if the rulers of this age had understood God's wisdom, they would not have crucified the Lord of glory. Paul is not saying that the Lord of glory is personified Wisdom. Rather, the apostle is stating that part of God's redemptive plan—God's wisdom that was "secret and hidden"—was the crucifixion of Christ.

It is in this light that 1 Corinthians 1:30 should be read: "And because of him you are in Christ Jesus, who became to us wisdom from God, righteousness and sanctification and redemption." What is at issue here is the gospel. Paul immediately defines how Christ has become wisdom to us from God by an enumeration of elements of the gospel: "righteousness, and sanctification, and redemption." Paul's wisdom teaching is not about identifying Christ with some antecedent figure, even tangentially, but about the entire drama of salvation as it is played out in Christ. Wisdom is in the crucifixion of Christ, with all of its implication for the church and the world, and with the proclamation of that message. This is the wisdom of God.

Paul's Trinitarian Framework

Paul's theology of wisdom and power in the context of 1 Corinthians 1 cannot be separated from Paul's underlying Trinitarian framework. In the next chapter, Paul explicitly relates the wisdom and power of God to the work of the Spirit (1 Cor. 2:1–16).

God the Holy Spirit. Paul reinforces his teaching about the nature of true wisdom and power in 1 Corinthians 2 by pointing

---

7. Fee, *Pauline Christology*, 102–3, goes so far as to say, "That is to talk nonsense, and it needs to be recognized as such. It is simply irresponsible to turn this pickup of the crucified Messiah in v. 23 into some form of identification with *personified* Jewish wisdom."

to his own ministry. In 1 Corinthians 2:1–5, he contrasts human wisdom with a gospel-oriented dependence on the power of God and the role of the Spirit. He did not minister at Corinth with lofty speech or wisdom. His focus was on a different kind of wisdom: "Jesus Christ and him crucified." Paul came with "weakness and in fear and much trembling." His speech and message were not "in plausible words of wisdom." On the contrary, Paul came "in demonstration of the Spirit and of power" so that the believers' faith "might not rest in the wisdom of men but in the power of God."

In 1 Corinthians 2:6–16, Paul contrasts human wisdom with God's wisdom and explains how God's wisdom is revealed by the Spirit. There is a true wisdom, unlike the wisdom of this age (1 Cor. 2:6). It is "a secret and hidden wisdom of God, which God decreed before the ages for our glory" (1 Cor. 2:7). The powers of the world did not understand this wisdom or they would not have "crucified the Lord of glory" (1 Cor. 2:8)—whose crucifixion, as we have seen, was at the heart of this wisdom (1 Cor. 1:23–24). This wisdom, which humans have never seen or heard or even imagined, had been prepared by God for his people (1 Cor. 2:9). It is the content of this wisdom that "God has revealed to us through the Spirit" (1 Cor. 2:10).[8]

The qualification of the Spirit to reveal divine wisdom points again to the inner life of the triune God. Jesus had said, "No one knows the Father except the Son" (Matt. 11:27). John echoed this qualification of the Son to reveal the Father (John 1:1, 18). Now Paul says, "No one comprehends the thoughts of God except the Spirit of God" (1 Cor. 2:11). Here are basic building blocks for the orthodox doctrine of the Trinity.

Again we are reminded how utterly dependent people are on God's self-revelation. This is why believers can rejoice, although not in their own wisdom; for "we have received not the spirit of the world, but the Spirit who is from God, that we might understand the things freely given us by God" (1 Cor. 2:12). This comes

8. The first of the nine gifts of the Spirit listed in 1 Corinthians 12:8–10 is "the utterance of wisdom."

not in words "taught by human wisdom but [words] taught by the Spirit" (1 Cor. 2:13). It is in the context of the triune God's self-revelation that we can grasp how this teaching on the Spirit echoes what Jesus taught when he said, "Take my yoke upon you, and learn from me" (Matt. 11:29). Salvation history moves forward from the life and ministry of Jesus, including his crucifixion and resurrection, to the coming of the Spirit at Pentecost in fulfillment of Jesus' promise. Jesus had taught that this Spirit would lead the church into all truth (John 16:12–14). Paul can now say that the "things of the Spirit of God" (1 Cor. 2:14) are "the mind of the Lord" and "the mind of Christ" (1 Cor. 2:16).[9]

God the Son. God is revealing himself in his Son. The Son uniquely shares in the life of the Father, pointing us to the Trinitarian shape of God's own being. God's self-revelation in his Son is counterintuitive: the wise and self-reliant of the world miss it; those who have a childlike faith receive it. Although often revealed in the context of rejection, those who respond begin to participate in salvation and share in the divine life. This revelation is defined by the gospel and the crucifixion of Christ. Here, added to the theme of revelation, is the theme of redemption.

It is the Spirit who applies this saving revelation in the life of the believer and the church, further teaching us about God's Son and drawing us into the life of the triune God (Titus 3:4–7). While these revelatory and redemptive themes have continuity with God's Word in the Old Testament, they transform the believer's relationship to the law: removing its burden and condemnation and replacing it with Christ and an inner transformation that accomplishes the law's divine intent (Gal. 4:4; Rom. 8:4).[10]

9. For another illustration of Paul's deeply Trinitarian understanding of God, see 1 Corinthians 12:1–11, which says that there is one Spirit, one Lord, and one God. Only by the Holy Spirit can one truly confess that "Jesus is Lord" (1 Cor. 12:3; see also Eph. 4:4–6).

10. Douglas Moo prefers to read Romans 8:4 as referring to the righteousness of Christ, rather than the righteousness of the Spirit fulfilled in the life of the believer; see his *The Epistle to the Romans*, New International Commentary on the New Testament (Grand Rapids: Eerdmans, 1996), 59–60. See also Robert A. Peterson, *Our Secure Salvation: Preservation and Apostasy* (Phillipsburg, NJ: P&R Publishing, 2009), 59–60. For the view taken above, see Kevin McFadden, "The Fulfillment of the Law's *Dikaioma*: Another Look

The Interplay of Wisdom Themes

Our Christological focus in this study is on Christ as God's wisdom. We are investigating this theme in the New Testament, and asking how this might apply in our lives as we seek to walk in the wisdom of God and be his people in the world. Each of the passages we are considering is unique, shaped by the author's particular purpose or set in the context of a specific problem. However, reading the New Testament's heightened Christological texts with attention, we hear the interplay of certain themes and their subthemes. Sometimes one motif is dominant, sometimes another; sometimes they combine as if the finale of a breathtaking symphony.

There is one theme to which we have not paid much attention, but that will begin to take a prominent place in the remainder of our study: the Son's role in creation. This role begins with the original creation, extends to power over the present fallen order, and climaxes in the creation's ultimate restoration in the new heaven and the new earth. In a passage often associated with Paul's identification of Christ as wisdom, both wisdom and power are implicitly combined in what may be Paul's most profound statement concerning the Son's role within the Godhead (1 Cor. 8:6). This text also illustrates the way Paul approaches pastoral problems with the wisdom of Christ, and serves as an application of 1 Corinthians 1:24.

1 Corinthians 8:6 as an Example of Wisdom Applied

This pivotal text in Paul introduces the cosmic theme of Christ's work: "yet for us there is one God, the Father, from whom are all things and for whom we exist, and one Lord, Jesus Christ, through whom are all things and through whom we exist" (1 Cor. 8:6). We saw this theme in John's prologue: "All things were

---

at Romans 8:1–4," *Journal of the Evangelical Theological Society* 52, 3 (September 2009): 483–97. If Moo's view is correct, the broader teaching of the New Testament on the work of the Spirit writing the law on the believer's heart makes the point.

made through him, and without him was not anything made that was made" (John 1:3). What makes Paul's text so important is its earlier date. John may well have been written toward the end of the first century. More liberal streams of scholarship would argue that John's high Christology, with Christ playing a role at the creation level, is a late development in the early church. Paul's statement here weighs against that claim, for 1 Corinthians was written much earlier, possibly in A.D. 55. Furthermore, this verse reads like a creed, and the way it is introduced without argumentation indicates that it may antedate Paul's composition, perhaps pushing the confession back into the 40s and the earliest days of the Christian church.

What connects this verse with our study, besides its astounding Christological affirmation and its ethical implications, is the suggestion that it is influenced by wisdom speculation. The argument goes like this. Since Paul identifies Christ with the Wisdom figure in 1 Corinthians 1:24 and 30, and since Wisdom is understood to be the mediator of creation in Jewish wisdom speculation, then 1 Corinthians 8:6 should naturally be read as transferring to Christ the role of Lady Wisdom at creation. Because we have rejected the assumption about the Wisdom figure identification in 1 Corinthians 1, the case for the connection in 1 Corinthians 8:6 is greatly weakened.[11]

The motif of Christ's creation role is an important Christological affirmation, and is related to God's wisdom as Paul and the New Testament portray it.[12] We need to look closer at 1 Corinthians 8:6, for it has important implications for how Paul is applying God's wisdom in practical terms to the situation at Corinth.

11. An analogy may be helpful here. The law was understood to be the locus of wisdom in intertestamental Judaism (e.g., Sirach), but for the New Testament writers, the law pointed forward to Christ, the true locus of wisdom. In a similar way, wisdom was understood to be personified in Lady Wisdom in the Old Testament and Second Temple Judaism; but for the early church, this figure at best served as a type, prefiguring Christ, the true embodiment of wisdom. In particular, Wisdom's role in creation can be seen as a type of Christ's role in creation. This much can be granted. However, one must be careful not to read this typology into New Testament passages without adequate textual warrant.

12. We will see this theme developed in our three remaining texts: Colossians 1:15–20; Philippians 2:5–11; and Hebrews 1:1–4.

"All Things"

Three questions help us get to the heart of what Paul is teaching in 1 Corinthians 8 with regard to Christ and wisdom. First, is Paul attributing to Christ a role in creation itself? Traditional exegesis has not hesitated to see the dogma of Christ's mediation at creation clearly affirmed in 1 Corinthians 8:6. Others have argued more recently that when Paul moves from "one God, the Father, from whom are all things and for whom we exist" to "one Lord, Jesus Christ, through whom are all things and through whom we exist," he is moving from God's creative work to Christ's redemptive work. In other words, all the created order comes from God, the Father, and all the things related to our salvation (but not the creation itself) come through Jesus Christ. But this is to tear apart what the New Testament consistently ties together; Christ's role in the created order is affirmed by various New Testament authors, most explicitly in John 1:3, Colossians 1:16, and Hebrews 1:2.

Furthermore, the language itself would have been recognized as having reference to the creation. Similar language, especially the expression "all things," is used both in first-century Stoicism and by the Jewish theologian Philo to speak of creation and its mediation from God through various agents. While Paul has a distinct theology of the Son as the Mediator, first-century readers would not have missed the reference to the creation.

Finally, Old Testament teaching confirms the traditional understanding of the text. God is commonly identified as the God of both creation and redemption. The two ideas are often associated within Old Testament literary structures. For example, Deuteronomy 10:14–22 refers to the God of creation (v. 14) and to the God of the exodus (vv. 19–22). At the center (v. 17) we read, "For the LORD your God is God of gods and Lord of lords, the great, the mighty, and the awesome God." This device of setting creation and redemption in juxtaposition is carried over into the New Testament.[13] Tying together Christ's cosmic and salvific roles will be important to Paul's pastoral point, and we will return to this below.

13. See the chapters on Colossians 1:15–20 and Hebrews 1:1–4.

71

The Son's Preexistence

In what sense does Paul see Christ as the Mediator of creation and of salvation? While Paul's language may reflect other first-century ideas about creation, the theological content of the New Testament pushes us far beyond Greek or Jewish philosophical ideas of mediation. If the cosmological significance of "all things" in 1 Corinthians 8:6 is granted, then it is difficult, if not impossible, to deny this as evidence for Paul's theology of Christ's preexistence. Furthermore, while the text may well be the earliest composition in the New Testament that explicitly confesses the Son's preexistence, the creedal way Paul expresses himself indicates that the concept was already present in the Christian community. This is confirmed by the fact that the Son's preexistence occurs in other confessional material such as Philippians 2:6–11.[14] Paul's declaration in 1 Corinthians 8:6 then provides an important building block for the orthodox doctrine of Christ's deity and the Trinitarian understanding of the Godhead. N. T. Wright sees 1 Corinthians 8:6 as a gloss on the *Shema* (Deut. 6:4), "a sort of Christological monotheism," or "a Christologically redefined monotheism."[15] Gordon Fee writes, "Although Paul does not here call Christ God, the formula is so constructed that only the most obdurate would deny its Trinitarian implications."[16]

This is, in part, why arguing that Paul is envisioning Christ in terms of the Jewish Wisdom figure falls short. Paul is identifying Christ more immediately with God, rather than with a personification of one of his attributes. Although it may use similar language, the New Testament has left far behind any Jewish speculation about the Wisdom figure, as well as other mediators. Instead, what we have is a "sonship" Christology. While a mix of Old Testament themes and elements from the life and ministry of Jesus inform New Testament Christology, what is central for Paul

14. See chap. 5.
15. N. T. Wright, "One God, One Lord, One People: Incarnational Christology for a Church in a Pagan Environment," *Ex auditu* 7 (1991): 48, 55.
16. Gordon D. Fee, *The First Epistle to the Corinthians* (Grand Rapids: Eerdmans, 1987), 375.

and for the New Testament writers in general is Christ's role as Son. This applies with reference to his work in creation as well. While the title "Son of God" is rare in Paul, it is present at both the beginning and end of 1 Corinthians.[17] Here in the confession of 1 Corinthians 8:6, "God" and "Lord" are defined by "Father" and "Jesus Christ," respectively. Although the term "Son" is not used, the filial relationship is implied by the use of the title "Father."

It may be interesting to ponder how Paul or the early church came to the conclusion that Jesus was a participant in creation. We may never be able to confirm such speculation with certainty. But it surely involved the early church's total experience of the Old Testament; the impact of the life, teaching, and ministry of Jesus; and the guidance of the Spirit. The proper background to understanding Christ's role in creation is complex. Not to be overlooked were the early traditions, known by the church, concerning Jesus' miraculous power over nature. The doctrine of Christ's role in creation need not be rooted solely, or even primarily, in an identification of Jesus with the personification of Wisdom, whether in the Old Testament or in later Jewish speculation. At the same time, it is not necessary to deny that reflection on personified Wisdom may have contributed in some way to the growing understanding on the part of Jesus' disciples and the early church as to Christ's identity and role in creation. However, this component ought not be exaggerated. The New Testament's explicit focus is on Christ as God's Son, and this will be confirmed in both Colossians and Hebrews.

Wisdom Applied

We have argued that the expression "all things" refers to creation and that Jesus' role in creation is to be understood primarily in terms of his sonship. But why does Paul quote this confessional material here in 1 Corinthians 8, and how *does* this relate to Christ and the gospel as wisdom? To answer this final question, we need to tie together Paul's pastoral approach in 1 Corinthians 1

17. See 1 Cor. 1:9; cf. "Father," 1:3; 15:24, 28.

with regard to the general problem of divisive claims to wisdom and Paul's pastoral approach in 1 Corinthians 8 to the particular problem of an inappropriate claim to knowledge.

The divisions and quarrels at Corinth appear to have stemmed in large measure from an overconfidence in human wisdom and the rhetorical power of words (1 Cor. 1:10–17). Paul responded to this by showing that true wisdom is found in the counterintuitive revelation and power of God located in Christ and the gospel (1 Cor. 1:18–31). Christ crucified is the wisdom and power of God (1 Cor. 1:24)! In this sense, the Father has made Jesus "our wisdom" (1 Cor. 1:30). The Spirit imparts this wisdom, granting believers the mind of Christ (2 Cor. 1–16), which includes correct understanding of the holiness and value of God's people as his temple (1 Cor. 3:16–17).

In 1 Corinthians 8, a specific example of such quarrels and divisions is dealt with, a problem that stemmed from a misunderstanding of "knowledge" (1 Cor. 8:1–4). Some, probably with a display of rhetorical flourish, were claiming that since we know there is only one God, then eating meat offered to idols is not a problem. An idol isn't anything, anyway (1 Cor. 8:4)! Some believers were proudly flaunting their liberty, even while other believers were being hurt (1 Cor. 8:7–13). It is in response to this misuse of knowledge that Paul inserts his confession about God and Christ (1 Cor. 8:6). While the "wise" at Corinth were affirming their monotheism ("there is no God but one" [1 Cor. 8:4]), Paul, in what turns out to be an amazing Christological affirmation, declares: "for us there is one God, the Father, from whom are all things and for whom we exist, and one Lord, Jesus Christ, through whom are all things, and through whom we exist" (1 Cor. 8:6). Yes, monotheism, or our belief in one God, rebuts idolatry. But since Christ and the gospel are now intimately related to how we understand God, to act with such "knowledge" while at the same time damaging a brother for whom Christ died is not consistent with true wisdom.

N. T. Wright insightfully comments, "In what is surely one of the most striking Christological formulations ever written . . .

74

Paul takes an argument which is about monotheism, and takes the Jewish formula, which is the most basic expression of Jewish monotheism, and places Jesus at the heart of it."[18] Paul does this without argumentation, and with the expectation that his readers will readily assent. This suggests how early the church confessed the most intimate association of the Son, in both his creation and redemption work, with the Father and God of Israel.

What Paul is adding, as it were, to this acknowledged confession is its immediate ethical implications. To walk in wisdom is now related, in every aspect of life, to Christ and the gospel. For the Corinthians this meant that the theological debate over the reality of idols and the practical question of eating meat offered to idols had to be framed in the context of the wisdom of Christ, the crucified one. As the church confesses the one true God, such a confession encompasses Christ—"through whom we exist"! So Paul writes that the "knowledgeable" at Corinth needed to remember that the weaker brother is one "for whom Christ died" (1 Cor. 8:11), and that to wound one's conscience in this matter was to "sin against Christ" (1 Cor. 8:12). Paul transitions instinctively from the most profound confession of Christology to the most practical matter of treating one another in a way consistent with the gospel.

Wisdom for Us

On the basis of our study, we can summarize our understanding of God's wisdom in Christ around three themes: revelation, redemption, and creation. Note how each of these has immediate practical implications for believers and the church.

Wisdom and Revelation

To know God and his wisdom, even in the limited way that is appropriate for finite human beings, is impossible—unless God

18. Wright, "One God, One Lord, One People," 48.

sovereignly reveals himself. We saw this in Jesus' prayer in Matthew 11:25–27: "I thank you, Father, Lord of heaven and earth, that you have hidden these things from the wise and understanding and revealed them to little children; yes, Father, for such was your gracious will." John's Gospel taught us the same lesson: those who participate in the transformative revelation of the Son, which makes them God's children, can do so only by the will of God (John 1:13). Apart from his self-revelation, we could never truly know God; but God, in the person of the Son, has graciously and wonderfully made him known to us (John 1:18).

Such an understanding of the unknowable God, who in the Son makes himself known, is Paul's teaching as well. In Galatians, Paul grounds his apostolic ministry in God's supernatural revelation (Gal. 1:1, 12). God called the apostle by his grace and was pleased to reveal his Son to Paul (Gal. 1:16). God sovereignly and graciously reveals himself, whether historically in the sending of the Son in the fullness of time (Gal. 4:4), or to Paul at his conversion and call to ministry (Gal. 1:1, 12, 16), or to you and me by the Holy Spirit (Gal. 4:6).

In Romans, Paul teaches that God's revelation has overcome barriers to knowing God and his ways. We are not to ask, "Who will ascend into heaven?" (Rom. 10:6). For God has revealed his will, first in the Old Testament (Deut. 30, especially vv. 11–14), and then climactically in the gospel of Christ, his Son (Rom. 10:6–13). Paul frames the entire Epistle to the Romans with this theology. The good news, promised in the Old Testament, and that concerns God's Son, has been revealed in the incarnation, resurrection, and proclamation of Jesus to all the nations (Rom. 1:1–6). The concluding doxology in Romans 16 describes Paul's gospel as

> the preaching of Jesus Christ, according to the revelation of the mystery that was kept secret for long ages but has now been disclosed and through the prophetic writings has been made known to all nations, according to the command of the eternal God, to bring about the obedience of faith. (Rom. 16:25b–26)

Here is the wisdom of God revealed. Paul's final words in Romans are: "to the only wise God be glory forevermore through Jesus Christ! Amen" (Rom. 16:27). When Paul describes God as "the only wise God," he is not thinking of "wisdom" as bare abstraction, but the wisdom of God as revealed particularly in the gospel. We find the same type of doxology in Romans 11. After discussing the wonderful way in which God both includes the Gentiles in the gospel and brings about the salvation of Israel (Rom. 11:1–32), Paul declares, "Oh, the depth of the riches and wisdom and knowledge of God! How unsearchable are his judgments and how inscrutable his ways!" (Rom. 11:33). We are absolutely dependent on God to reveal his wisdom. We cannot reach it by our own efforts; but in these last days God has wonderfully revealed this wisdom to us in Christ and the gospel.

How strange it is, then, for us as Christians to treat one another with intellectual pride—turning our mental acumen against one another, flaunting our educational achievements, or trusting in our ability to win a theological argument! Rigorous conversations about the gospel, about what the Bible means, or about how we are to live out the faith surely please God. But what irony when this deteriorates into a divisive spirit and broken relationships! This is not the wisdom from above. As children of the kingdom, we need to repent. What we know of truth is a generous gift from our heavenly Father. Our growth in God's wisdom is still utterly dependent on the Spirit of Christ who leads us into all truth.

Paul's purpose in using the wisdom language of Christ in 1 Corinthians 1:24 and 30 was to deal with this kind of pride and divisiveness. There are two other lessons that we can take away from the way God's wisdom is revealed in Christ. First, God's wisdom can be rejected and distorted; and second, God's wisdom is revealed to the humble and broken.

Throughout our study we have seen God's wisdom refused. This is a result of several factors: the fragmented and limited nature of human understanding, the effects of the fall, and the unique nature of God's wisdom. Christ's wisdom can be rejected in various ways. The rejection can stem from unbelief in Christ and his mission (Matt. 11:19–20; John 1:11). But it can also be a more subtle rejection. At Corinth it took the form of a practical denial of truth within the community—one that stemmed from misunderstanding how God's wisdom works. Such a distortion is characterized by overconfidence in human wisdom and a worldly understanding of power.

The distortion of God's wisdom narrows the field of those who can fully enjoy God's revelation. It has been all too common in the history of the church for leaders to impose unnecessary requirements on God's people. The result is spiritual bondage. Are there ways in which we too have fallen under such slavery? Do we impose on others religious standards that deny the gospel? We should not vindicate ourselves too quickly.

It has also been common to exclude some from full fellowship because they fall short in sophisticated theological reasoning. The result is divisiveness in the body of Christ. The line between what the Lord requires of us and what are merely inappropriate burdens requires discernment. Likewise, the line between the true treasures of the gospel and complicated but unhealthy theological constructs can get blurry. It is dangerous when we confuse our love for truth with an unhealthy confidence that we already possess the truth. The proper response is to make sure we remain humble and teachable before the God of all wisdom.

Second, we have learned that God's wisdom is revealed to the humble and broken. We should not make the mistake of thinking that the New Testament's orientation toward the poor and weak is simply an accommodation to its original audience. It is true that Jesus' first audience, as well as the majority of the church at Corinth, was poor and weak. But this is where God chooses to reveal himself, and it is still true today. God reveals himself to the poor and marginalized: this is embedded in the nature of God's love and salvation—and in the wisdom of the gospel. Jesus invited the poor, the little children, those who were weary and heavy laden. Paul describes those called and being saved as the lowly and despised (1 Cor. 1:26–31). Here is where the wisdom and love of God is most often revealed.

Wisdom and Redemption

When Christ invited people to be his disciples and to enter his school of wisdom (Matt. 11:28–29), he knew this would lead them to the cross. This is implied when Jesus reminded his disciples, "Whoever does not take his cross and follow me is not worthy of me" (Matt. 10:38) and "If anyone would come after me, let him deny himself and take up his cross and follow me" (Matt. 16:24). The Christian life is a cruciform life, shaped by the way of the cross. However, its foundation and the fount of its wisdom are not in *our* cross-bearing, but in the unique and saving cross-bearing of Christ.

In 1 Corinthians 2:7–8, Paul teaches us that the hidden and secret wisdom of God involves the crucifixion of "the Lord of glory." The conjoining of crucifixion and glory does not make sense to human wisdom, but it *is* God's wisdom. John, in his prologue, taught us that when the Word became flesh, his followers saw "his glory, glory as of the only Son from the Father, full of grace and truth" (John 1:14). The connection between this glory and the crucifixion is brought out later in John when Jesus says, "The hour has come for the Son of Man to be glorified," and he goes on to speak of his crucifixion (John 12:23–24, 32–33).

The wisdom of Christ takes us to the foot of the cross, where by faith we can become children of God (John 1:12). Here we find that "Christ is the end of the law for righteousness to everyone who believes" (Rom. 10:4), as we confess that Jesus is Lord, and believe in our hearts that the Father "raised him from the dead" (Rom. 10:9). Here we become God's sons and heirs, as we are redeemed from the law by Christ and taught to cry "Abba! Father!" by the Spirit (Gal. 4:5–7).

For the apostle, God's wisdom is found in the plan of salvation that reaches its culmination at the cross of Christ. When Paul calls Christ "the wisdom of God and the power of God"

79

(1 Cor. 1:24), he is speaking of the cross and Christ crucified; he is speaking of the gospel. The secret and hidden wisdom of God, which is now revealed, is the crucifixion of Christ (1 Cor. 2:7), with all that this means for the church and the world. Any wisdom that is not ultimately cross-oriented is not true wisdom. This is why Paul's singular "knowledge" when he came to Corinth was "Jesus Christ and him crucified" (1 Cor. 2:2). This is the nature of the wisdom that we learn in Jesus' school of discipleship (Matt. 11:29). This is what it means to "have the mind of Christ" (1 Cor. 2:16) and to have the wisdom of God revealed to us by the Spirit (1 Cor. 2:7, 10). In all three of our final passages (Col. 1:15–20; Phil. 2:5–11; and Heb. 1:1–4), the centrality of the cross and its redemptive power will be emphasized.

The person who is characterized by the wisdom of God will respond in humility and childlike faith to the Father's revelation in the Son. He or she will identify and care for the poor and broken even as Jesus did, and such a person will both experience and proclaim to others God's redemption from sin through faith in Christ's finished work on the cross.

Wisdom and Creation

In case we think that the focus on Christ and his crucifixion is too narrow a foundation for wisdom, we need to follow the New Testament further into the depths of its Christology. The person and work of Christ lead us, in breathtaking fashion, into the life of the triune God and then to the restoration of the whole creation. The gospel and the cross are anchored in the Trinity by the Son's unique relationship to the Father and the Spirit. This has implications that are at once intensely practical and yet beyond our final comprehension.

Jesus claimed an enclosed life of intimate knowledge with the Father (Matt. 11:27). John celebrated this common life and mutual identity that Jesus shared with God the Father (John 1:1, 18). He also revealed how all things were made through Christ, as the Word (John 1:3, 10). Paul, in clarifying the relationship between the gospel and the law, assumed that the Son came from the Father into the created order (Rom. 10:6; Gal. 4:4) and is "Lord of all" (Rom. 10:9, 12–13).

In 1 Corinthians 8:6, Paul in creedal fashion gathered these Trinitarian and cosmic dimensions together as he confessed: "There is one God, the Father, from whom are all things and for whom we exist, and one Lord, Jesus Christ, through whom are all things and through whom we exist." What is most profound is the way Paul applied this astonishing confession to the practical matter of caring for one another. We should live for one another, as those for whom Christ died. Here is the cure to divisiveness among God's people.

The wisdom of God turns us away from our own wisdom to the way of Christ and the cross, to a life characterized by humility, unity, and mutual service, and then to a glorious vision of the restoration of the whole created order. We will catch a glimpse of this cosmic reconciliation as we study Colossians in our next chapter.

4

Wisdom and the Cosmic Christ (Colossians 1:15-20)

He is the image of the invisible God, the firstborn of all creation. For by him all things were created, in heaven and on earth, visible and invisible, whether thrones or dominions or rulers or authorities—all things were created through him and for him. And he is before all things, and in him all things hold together. And he is the head of the body, the church. He is the beginning, the firstborn from the dead, that in everything he might be preeminent. For in him all the fullness of God was pleased to dwell, and through him to reconcile to himself all things, whether on earth or in heaven, making peace by the blood of his cross.

Introduction

On January 17, 1991, when the first Gulf War in Iraq began, Saddam Hussein said it would be the "Mother of all Battles." A dozen years later the United States described its strategy at the beginning of the second Iraq conflict as "shock and awe"—a military tactic using overwhelming power and spectacular force to paralyze an enemy and destroy its will to fight. The exercise of human power can be frightening. Supernatural power can be even more terrifying. In a fallen world, such powers can paralyze and destroy, both physically and spiritually. The New Testament calls this grip of evil "the domain of darkness" (Col. 1:13).

83

Hope can be found only in a greater power. In the kingdom of God's beloved Son, we meet a sovereign who has authority over the entire created order and even over death. His is the only power that can reconcile the world, subdue evil, and bring peace.

Paul celebrates this power in Colossians 1:15–20—one of the most concentrated Christological passages in the New Testament—which poetically sums up the wisdom of God in Christ. It focuses on all three of the grand themes concerning the Son of God: revelation, creation, and redemption. As with 1 Corinthians 8:6, this passage has the feel of a confession, and it amplifies the theme of Christ as the agent of creation that we saw in 1 Corinthians. There are multiple bridges, both conceptual and structural, between Colossians 1:15–20 and Hebrews 1:1–4; not least of these connections is the focus on Christ in his creation role. There are also important connections between Colossians and Ephesians, where the apostle makes an instinctive move from a focus on Christ as Creator to a focus on the implications of this Christology for the church.[1]

A look at three preliminary questions about Paul and the situation at Colossae prepares us for the message of this passage. Then we will examine the text's structure, along with its theology.

- Preliminary Questions
- The Son and the Poetic Structure of Colossians 1:15–20
- God's Son as Creator (Part 1, Colossians 1:15–16)
- God's Son as Absolute Center (Part 2, Colossians 1:17–18a)
- God's Son as Reconciler (Part 3, Colossians 1:18b–20)
- Summary and Application of the Wisdom in Christ

Preliminary Questions

Authorship

Some modern scholars have questioned whether Paul wrote Colossians. However, the confessing church has historically

---

1. While not included in this study, Ephesians 2:14–16 merits special attention as a Christological text with a concentrated focus on the church.

and universally accepted Pauline authorship, and there is no need to call this into question.[2] The theology of Colossians is consistent with what Paul teaches elsewhere; and as we will see, this certainly holds for its Christology. There is a unique emphasis in Colossians, and in part this is what leads some to question the epistle's authorship. This should alert us to the special way in which the apostle applies his Christology to the problems at Colossae.

A slightly more difficult question concerns the composition of Colossians 1:15–20. Again, some have argued that Paul adapts a traditional hymnic or poetic fragment, inserting this preexisting material into his epistle. While there is nothing about the orthodox doctrine of Scripture that rules out this possibility, the claim remains speculative. Even if it is conceded that this is hymnic material, there is no reason why Paul could not have composed it to fit his rhetorical purpose in Colossians. Many scholars prefer to call this "poetic" material. At least we need to be alert that we are dealing with a heightened literary style in these verses, one that Paul uses to help communicate his message about Christ for the Colossian believers.[3]

The Colossian Problem

This brings us to a final preliminary question. What is the problem at Colossae? Paul's purpose is to confirm the believers in the gospel (Col. 1:6; 2:6–7) and to assure them of their salvation (1:13–14, 20, 22). The apostle wants them to be encouraged, to be united in love, and to reach a fuller understanding of God's wisdom in Christ (2:2–3). He is writing so that they will not be deluded "with plausible arguments" (2:4). But what are these arguments?

There is no consensus among scholars about what has come to be known as the "Colossian heresy." While we may not be able

---

2. Recently there has been a growing consensus even among more liberal scholars that Paul is the probable author of the epistle; see Christian Stettler, "The Opponents at Colossae," in *Paul and His Opponents*, Pauline Studies, vol. 5, ed. Stanley Porter (Boston: Brill, 2005), 169.

3. For further discussion of hymns in the worship of the early church, see chapter 5.

to answer the question conclusively, the issue does have a bearing on our study. First, whatever the problem threatening the church, Paul teaches us that God's wisdom in Christ is the answer. Second, it is yet another reminder that God's self-revelation is always attended by belief *and* by rejection and opposition. Wrestling with the errors faced by the Colossian church, along with Paul's Christological solution, can help prepare us to face conflict in our own day.

Most agree that the false teaching comes primarily from the surrounding community of unbelievers, although the social relationships between believers and those outside the church were undoubtedly complex. A good case can be made that it was a mosaic of religious ideas, a kind of syncretism of pagan, Jewish, and Christian ideas and practices.[4] While such a view of the heresy is increasingly popular among commentators, a strong case can also be made for locating the problem in the local Jewish synagogue.[5] This is an older view that still has merit. It is helpful to focus on the explicit statements about the dangers that the Colossians face, in order to see the contours of the opposition. From these texts we can list the characteristics of the "Colossian heresy."[6]

Introduction to the Opposition (Colossians 2:4, 8). Their "plausible words," with which they would delude the believers (Col. 2:4), are described as "philosophy and empty deceit" or "a would-be wisdom that is hollow deception" (2:8). This agrees with the later expression, "an appearance of wisdom" (2:23). The "wise" at Corinth and the "philosophers" at Athens (Acts 17:18) were Greeks. At Colossae we may have a Jewish claim, under the influence of Greek culture, to philosophical wisdom. The term "philosophy" suggests that it is a relatively coherent system. Paul calls it "human tradition" (Col. 2:8).

4. See C. E. Arnold, *The Colossian Syncretism: The Interface between Christianity and Folk Belief at Colossae* (Grand Rapids: Baker, 1996).

5. Stettler, "The Opponents at Colossae," 169–200. My summary of the problem at Colossae is largely dependent on Stettler's study. For a similar approach with slightly different conclusions, see the judicious treatment in Douglas Moo, *The Letter to the Colossians and to Philemon*, Pillar New Testament Commentary (Grand Rapids: Eerdmans, 2008).

6. These come primarily in Colossians 2:4, 8, 16–17a, 18, and 20–23.

Practices of the Opposition (Colossians 2:16–17a). Their practices, with which they passed judgment on the Christians, were characterized by the old era, and were "a shadow of the things to come" (Col. 2:17), namely, rules about food, drink, festivals, new moons, or the Sabbath (2:16). These are Jewish practices, and while they are largely rooted in the Old Testament, their proponents had failed to recognize the forward movement in redemptive history. They were clinging to the shadow, while the substance had already come, which is Christ.[7]

Experiences of the Opposition (Colossians 2:18). Their religious experiences, with which they would disqualify the followers of Christ, involved ascetic practices.[8] These included fasting and mystic visions by which they peered into angelic worship (Col. 2:18). It is known that early Jewish mystics had an interest in the heavenly worship conducted by the angels.[9] Paul argues that their motives are not truly spiritual, which is evidenced by the fact that they do not hold to Christ (2:19). This expression does not imply that the false teachers were inside the community. Paul's tone for false brethren is more severe, as, for example, in Galatians.

Summary of the Opposition (Colossians 2:20–23). Paul repeats his identification of the errors at Colossae, as he combines and summarizes the practices and experiences already noted in 2:16–18. The practices involve Jewish regulations: do not handle, do not taste, and do not touch! These are related to the rules about food and drink mentioned in Colossians 2:16. Paul had called these shadows of the old dispensation (2:17), and now describes them as related to the elements of the world (2:20), by which Paul means the old age that is now passing away. The experiences, which

7. The meaning is close to Hebrews 8:5 and 10:1.

8. The word translated "asceticism" in Col. 2:18 is translated "humility" in Colossians 3:12. It has a technical meaning related to fasting as a special expression of humility (Col. 2:18) and a more common usage for the virtue of humility (Col. 3:18).

9. The phrase "worship of angels" (Col. 2:18) can be translated as "angelic worship," or the worship that angels offer. What would develop in the Middle Ages as the Jewish mysticism known as Kaballah ("received, handed down") had roots going back to pre-New Testament times. Kabbalistic literature speculated about Enoch and Elijah (Gen. 5:24; 2 Kings 2:11), who both ascended to heaven, and about the Lord's throne (*merkabah*) and the surrounding angels (cf. Isa. 6:2).

project an appearance of wisdom, involve "self-made religion and asceticism and severity to the body" that stem from the Jewish mystics' interest in angelic worship (2:23).

There may have been a degree of religious syncretism in the Jewish community at Colossae, but the primary theological and religious threat to the earliest Christian community as a whole was the reaction from Judaism. This seems to be the case at Colossae as well. Those who might delude (2:4), take captive (2:8), pass judgment on (2:16), and disqualify (2:18) the fledgling Christian community tended to be those in the Jewish community who had not accepted Christ and the gospel. When we understand the Colossian error from these explicit statements, then other components of Paul's epistle make sense. For example, the repeated references to "circumcision" and "uncircumcision" are probably not incidental, but directed against the local opposition (2:11, 13; 3:11).

Whether this is the correct reading of the "Colossian heresy" or not, one thing is clear: at every turn Paul's response is to point the believers to Christ. Those who would take the Colossians captive are not in line with Christ, in whom the fullness of deity dwells bodily (2:8–9). In response to those who would delude the Christians (2:4), Paul calls for firmness of "faith in Christ" (2:5), "in whom are hidden all the treasures of wisdom and knowledge" (2:3). The problem with those who are passing judgment on the believers (2:16) is that they are not holding to the Head, who is Christ (2:19). Finally, when Paul summarizes the error (2:20–23) of legal regulations and the asceticism related to the worship of angels, he emphasizes the believers' identification with Christ in his death and resurrection (2:20; 3:1). The health of the church can best be measured by how well it lives up to a sound Christology. Paul's challenge to the church is well expressed in Colossians 2:6: "Therefore as you received Christ Jesus the Lord, so walk in him."

To prepare for this apologetic purpose and pastoral counsel to the Colossians, the apostle presents his wonderful poem of praise to Christ in Colossians 1:15–20. The apostle gathers up many of the Christological themes we have already seen, weaving them together in an original and artistic fashion, all with the purpose of addressing the needs of the church. The framework for the unit is provided on one side by Colossians 1:12–14, which is a kind of overture that prepares for the words of praise, with its themes taken up again in the poem. The framework is closed by Colossians 1:21–23, which proceeds to draw out the implications for the readers. The references to Christ in the apologetic section (1:24–2:23) then build off the Christology celebrated in Colossians 1:15–20.

The Son and the Poetic Structure of Colossians 1:15-20

The Poetic Structure. Examining the structure of Paul's composition helps us to catch important nuances of its Christology. The poem has three stanzas. The first part, on Christ and creation (Col. 1:15–16), is balanced by the third part, on Christ and reconciliation (1:18b–20). The center holds the poem together by confessing Christ's dual authority over all things in creation and over his body, the church (1:17–18a). The text, following the ESV, with a slight revision at the end, is laid out below:

> *He is* the image of the invisible God,
> *the firstborn* of all creation.
> *For by him* all things were **created**,
>   in heaven and on earth,
>   visible and invisible,
>   whether thrones or dominions
>   or rulers or authorities—
> all things were **created** *through* him and *for* him.
>
> And he is before all things,
>   and in him all things hold together.
> And he is the head of the body, the church.
>
> *He is* the beginning,
> *the firstborn* from the dead,
> that in everything he might be preeminent.
> *For in him* all the fullness of God was pleased to dwell,

and *through* him to **reconcile** *to* himself all things,
   making peace by the blood of his cross,
[**to reconcile** all things] through him
   whether on earth or in heaven.[10]

The best place to begin examining Paul's poem is at the center (Col. 1:17–18a), which plays a critical role in the composition. The formal criteria for seeing these three lines as the central axis are clear. Notice the balance of the wording:

And he is before all things,
   and in him all things hold together.
And he is the head of the body, the church.

The "all things" in the first line of this central core, over which Christ has authority (1:17a), refers to the "creation" of the first section (1:15–16). The phrase in the third line, "the body, the church," which is the object of Christ's headship (1:18a), refers to the redemption of the final section (1:18b–20). The three lines of this center are then surrounded by the two balancing sections (1:15–16 and 1:18b–20), each consisting of eight lines, and each beginning with the words "He is" (or translated more literally, "Who is"). The skeleton of the structure is as follows:

Who is . . .
And he is
   And in him all things hold together
And he is
Who is . . .

This places the phrase "and in him all things hold together" at the very center of both the middle section and the entire poem. The center line's structural function (holding the poetic compo-

---

10. The ESV drops the second "through him" line and inverts the order of the remaining last two clauses for stylistic reasons. To examine the poem's structure, the end of the poem has been translated following the Greek order, and words that are to be assumed by the reader are placed in brackets before the second "through him" in verse 20.

sition together) is actually a literary portrayal of its theological content: Christ holds everything together (both creation and new creation). This is truly art to the glory of God, and sound theology for our personal lives and for the church. God's Son, our Lord Jesus Christ, is "the center"—the one in whom all reality holds together. This is the message that the Colossians needed. This is the timeless message that we need.

Let us turn now to consider the two surrounding units. There are several literary features that function to hold these sections together, marking them as parallel to one another and distinguishing them from the context.[11] There are three formal elements that are important. First, both the first and last units are built around the three introductory expressions:

> He (or Who) is . . .
> the firstborn . . .
> For in him . . .[12]

(We have italicized these words in the layout of the complete poem above so that they can easily be seen.) Second, both units make comprehensive statements about Christ's creative work or his work of reconciliation by using the same series of three distinct prepositions. In the first unit, Paul announces that all things were created "by," "through," and "for" Christ (1:16). In the second unit, Paul declares that all things were reconciled "in," "through," and "to" Christ (1:19–20). Although translated differently for English style, the same set of Greek prepositions is used; the second set echoes the first. (We have italicized these prepositions in the layout above so that they can be identified.) This is language typically used of God's relationship to creation and redemption. We saw this in 1 Corinthians 8:6, where Christ

11. The first section of eight lines has 44 words in the Greek, the last section of eight lines has 48 words, and the middle section of three lines has 20 words. This shows the general symmetry of the poem.

12. Both lines read "in him" in the Greek, but the ESV translates the first phrase as "by him" and the second as "in him." This is good English style, but makes it more difficult to see the complete parallelism.

is confessed within the context of God's creative and redemptive work. In Colossians, Paul amplifies that confession.

The final formal feature, which shows the symmetry of the first and last units of Paul's poetic praise to Christ, is a double reference to the act of creation in the first section (1:16) and a double reference to reconciliation in the second section (1:20). These verbs are presented in bold letters in the layout above.[13] The words between the doublets amplify the comprehensiveness of the Son's creative work ("in heaven and on earth" [1:16]), and then the means of the Son's saving work ("making peace by the blood of his cross" [1:20]). Paul concludes his poem with a final reference to "on earth and in heaven," both of which are encompassed by Christ's reconciliation. He does this in inverted order (1:16 has "in heaven and on earth"), which is a final literary device that closes the poem and stresses the cosmic totality of Christ's victory.

The precise balance of the first and last units is significantly disturbed by the clause "that in everything he might be preeminent" (1:18). Perfect symmetry is not the intention of such poetic or hymnic structures. Form and content are in a certain purposeful tension. The structural pattern is set in the first unit (1:15–16a): "He is . . . the firstborn . . . For in him . . ." But in the second unit the echo of the final part ("For in him . . .") is delayed to emphasize a point. This point was anticipated in the transition stanza (1:17–18a), but must now be made explicit: not only is the Son first in regard to creation, but through the resurrection (as the climax of his work on the cross), he has become *in everything* preeminent. Christ is first not only in the created universe, but also in the church. The apostle takes a deep breath with this clause and is now about to rush forward to the climax of the poem, which is the crucifixion of Christ and reconciliation. Form partly gives way to content, but the point is made: Christ is all in all!

---

13. This second doublet is often missed by scholars, or left out in translation, because it is only implied by the repetition of the phrase "through him," and must be supplied mentally by the reader. At this point Paul is less concerned with explicit symmetry, and more concerned with his theology of the cross, although the poem rounds off nicely.

Christ's Identity as the Son. Nearly everywhere in the New Testament narratives about Christ, we find that the subject is the Son of God. In the Christological poem in Colossians, the personal identity of the one praised is introduced explicitly as God's beloved Son (Col. 1:13). This fundamental assumption of New Testament Christology must guide any discussion of the wisdom of God in Christ. The subject is not wisdom, which finds residence in Christ; rather, the focus is on the Son of God, in whose person and work God's wisdom is found. Striking a balance here is important. On the one hand, we should not exaggerate the role of personified Wisdom, either as the Wisdom figure or in the so-called Wisdom story's influence on the gospel narrative.[14] On the other hand, we should not neglect God's final and full self-revelation in his own Son, which is identified in the New Testament as God's very wisdom.

While describing God's revelation and work in his Son, it is true that some of the language used elsewhere of personified Wisdom is applied to Christ. However, we should remember two important facts. First, this language is also used elsewhere of other agencies, such as the law and the Word. And second, this language is being used in ways that far exceed the way it is used of Wisdom. This will be illustrated as we look carefully at what is said about Christ as God's Son, first in relationship to the creation and then in relationship to the church. Such a comparison will also focus our attention on the heights of Paul's Christology in Colossians 1:15–20. It will be helpful to organize our treatment around the three-part structure of Paul's composition.

God's Son as Creator (Part 1, Colossians 1:15-16)

Image of the Invisible God (Colossians 1:15)

The Son is "the image of the invisible God" (Col. 1:15)—this is the first thing that Paul tells us about the Son in his poem. In

14. Interpreters err when they assume a pre-New Testament narrative about Wisdom, as if there were a coherent Jewish account about Wisdom as one who comes to earth, accomplishes salvation, and returns to heaven.

Wisdom of Solomon 7:26, a Jewish work from the time between the Testaments, wisdom is called "an image of the goodness of God." The similarities are impressive, but so are the differences. The Greek term translated "image" can be understood as a metaphor signifying "revelation," but depending on the context it may also involve substantial participation in the object revealed.[15] Wisdom in Pseudo-Solomon is described as revealing various attributes of God; in Wisdom 7:26 it is his "goodness." But the Son in Colossians 1:15 is described as one who reveals God himself (God being qualified simply as invisible or unseen). This is a significant difference. The apostle's focus is on the Son's revelation of God through the incarnation and the gospel, but Paul is assuming the preexistence of the Son. He is one who is fully qualified to reveal the Father, because he participates in the divine nature. It is this participation in the divine nature that enables the Son to be first the agent of creation and also the revealer of the Father. This is the one who can truly show us God (cf. Matt. 11:27; John 1:1, 18). What Paul means is brought out in Colossians 1:19 and more fully in Colossians 2:9. In the Son "all the fullness of God was pleased to dwell," and "in him the whole fullness of deity dwells bodily." This is close to Paul's usage in 2 Corinthians, where the apostle speaks of the glory of Christ, "who is the image of God" (2 Cor. 4:4). God has revealed himself in Christ that we might have "the knowledge of the glory of God in the face of Jesus Christ" (2 Cor. 4:6). The Son as the image of God is more than a revelation of God's wisdom; he is a revelation of God himself.

The identity of the Son as the "image" of the Father, while encompassing the Son's preexistence and role in creation, is also related to the Son's incarnational work, in which the Son embodies the image of God as the second Adam. This will have practical implications for the application of wisdom in the life of the church.

15. Markus Barth and Helmut Blanke, *Colossians: A New Translation with Introduction and Commentary*, Anchor Bible Commentary (New York: Doubleday, 1995), 195.

Firstborn of All Creation (Colossians 1:15)

Proverbs 8 represents personified Wisdom as present with God at creation: "when he established the heavens I [Wisdom] was there . . . When he marked out the foundations of the earth, then I was beside him" (Prov. 8:27, 29). Wisdom 9:9 repeats this idea: "now with you is Wisdom, who knows your works and was present when you made the world."[16] These texts, which figuratively describe the attribute of God's wisdom as a person, speak of wisdom's priority to the creation. Before the creation existed, God's wisdom existed. Yet these texts also speak, again metaphorically, of God's bringing forth his wisdom or even creating it (Prov. 8:23).[17] This is not to suggest that there was a time before God was wise. In the execution of his plan to bring forth the created order, the plan itself is visualized as shaped first. Here, of course, human language groans to speak about the deep things of God. The point seems to be that as we move from eternity past into the realm of created history, what comes first, even before creation, is God's wise plan and purposes.

However, with regard to the Son as the "firstborn" of all creation, Paul is speaking of more than temporal priority. While Christ's preexistence is assumed, the emphasis of the term "firstborn" is on the superior rank of the messianic Son. The background for Paul's use of the term "firstborn" includes such messianic texts as Psalm 89:27 and 2 Samuel 7:12–17. These texts are taken up in Hebrews 1:5–6, where "Son" and "firstborn" are synonymous titles. Christ has the inheritance rights, as the Son of God and Messiah, over the entire created order (Heb. 1:2). This is not something ever said of personified Wisdom, but it is God's wisdom for us in Christ. The whole created order, both the universe and the church, is under the authority of God's Son.[18]

16. All quotations of the Apocrypha in this chapter are from the *New American Bible*.

17. Cf. Sir. 24:9: "Before all ages, in the beginning, he created me, and through all ages I shall not cease to be."

18. For a helpful study on the use of "firstborn" in Colossians 1:15, see Larry R. Helyer, "Arius Revisited: The Firstborn over All Creation (Col 1:15)," *Journal of the Evangelical Theological Society* 31, 1 (March 1, 1988): 59–67.

"Agent" of Creation (Colossians 1:16)

Paul now celebrates Christ's role in creation. Everything was created by him; this includes every aspect of reality, and it all was created through him and for him (Col. 1:16). As we have seen, the Old Testament and other Jewish works unquestionably assign a role in creation to Wisdom. This has its roots in Proverbs 8, where Wisdom is beside the Lord at creation "like a master workman" (Prov. 8:30). Pseudo-Solomon declares that Wisdom is "the artificer of all."[19] But it is a mistake to draw too close an identification between a Wisdom figure and Christ. The personification of Wisdom is metaphorical language used to describe God's wisdom at creation (Prov. 3:19), and so the idea of Wisdom as a person should not be exaggerated. Furthermore, as we have seen, several other agents are associated in Jewish literature with this role in creation.

What is said here of the Son in relation to creation goes far beyond what is ever said of Wisdom, and relates both to the Son's deity and to his messianic role. This can be seen in the three distinct prepositions that describe the Son's comprehensive relationship to creation. The phrase translated "by him" (Col. 1:16) is from the Greek phrase better rendered "in him."[20] It refers to the sphere in which creation takes place, much like God's election takes place "in Christ" (Eph. 1:4).[21] In other words, this phrase is not simply a variation of what comes later ("all things were created through him" [Col. 1:16]). The Son's role in relationship to creation is more comprehensive than that of an agent. The point is that all things were created "in connection with the Son." The last two prepositional phrases in the verse then bring out particular aspects of this more comprehensive connection, stressing agency and purpose: "all things were created through him and for him." The universe is created in Christ, by Christ, and ultimately for Christ.

19. Cf. Wisd.. 8:5, 6; 14:2.
20. See the footnote in the ESV that gives this as an alternative translation.
21. Peter T. O'Brien, *Colossians, Philemon*, Word Biblical Commentary (Waco, TX: Word, 1982), 45.

When Paul concludes this verse by confessing that all things were created "for him," the apostle signifies that Christ is the goal of creation (Col. 1:16). This concept finds no parallel in Jewish literature related to the Wisdom figure. In 1 Corinthians 8:6, this phrase is used of God himself, showing how easily Paul can move from Christ to God and vice versa. Two profound truths are interwoven in these phrases: the intimate association, even identification, of the Son with God; and, at the same time, the identity of the Son in his messianic role. Neither element in this pair should be neglected. The Son is the "image" (Col. 1:15) not merely of an attribute of God, but of God himself; yet as the second Adam, Christ is also the image of God in his incarnation, where all the fullness of God dwells bodily (Col. 2:9). The Son in his deity is the goal of the created order (1 Cor. 8:6); in God's wisdom, reaching this goal entails Christ's role as the messianic heir of all things. This was implied in the term "firstborn," where the Son has the inheritance rights over creation. As the author of Hebrews teaches, the Son's appointment as "heir of all" is linked with Christ's role as the one "through whom the Father created the world" (Heb. 1:2). The creation purpose terminates in the messianic Son.

God's Son as Absolute Center (Part 2, Colossians 1:17–18a)

Ruler of Creation (Colossians 1:17)

Paul says that the Son is "before all things" (Col. 1:17). This could be a reference to either the Son's temporal priority to creation or the Son's superior status over the creation. These are not mutually exclusive—the phrase may be intentionally vague to encompass both; that is, the Son, as the Son and agent of creation, existed before anything was created, and therefore has a sovereign right over the creation.

Any comparison here with the Wisdom figure only serves to highlight the depth of Paul's Christology. In Proverbs 8:23–26, we are told that Wisdom was brought forth "before" the Lord created the earth and the mountains and the fields, etc. The apocryphal

Sirach says that "before all things . . . wisdom was created" and "before all ages, in the beginning, he created me [i.e., wisdom]" (Sir. 1:4; 24:9). Two key differences stand out when we compare this with what Paul and the New Testament say of Christ. First, the Son was never "brought forth" (Proverbs) or "created" (Sirach); he is the eternal Son. Second, the Son in the context of the Colossian hymn is not only "before" temporally, but "before" as the sovereign ruler. This interpretation is confirmed by the analysis of the structure. It is this line ("he is before all things") that summarizes the messianic Son's authoritative rule over the created order, particularly in his capacity as Creator.

Sustaining Center of All (Colossians 1:17)

At the center of his poetic account, Paul declares that "in him (i.e., the Son) all things hold together" (Col. 1:17). Clearly, God himself is the one who holds all things together. Greek philosophers recognized this. A second-century philosophical work written in North Africa has the clearest parallel to Paul's language: "all things are from God and through God [all things] hold together."[22] Parallels in ancient Jewish literature, however, are closer to New Testament theology. It is the Spirit of the Lord who has filled the world and "holds all things together" (Wisd. 1:7). When Pseudo-Solomon tells us that Wisdom "renews all things" (Wisd. 7:27) and "orders all things well" (Wisd. 8:1), this is a way of speaking of God's general providential care of the creation. Yet Paul is saying something more of Christ.

What is said in Colossians of the Son, in keeping with the language and the poetic structure, confesses Christ as the sustainer of creation, but goes beyond this: he is the one in whom all, including both creation and redemption, have their unifying principle, their center of integration. This is not merely a reference to raw power, but to meaning and redemptive purpose—to divine wisdom itself. At the center of the prologue to Hebrews is the similar confession: the Son in the context of his saving work

22. Cf. O'Brien, *Colossians*, 47.

"upholds the universe by the word of his power" (Heb. 1:3). We need to hold together what Paul does in his poem: first, everything was created "in connection with the Son" (Col. 1:16); second, the incarnation for the purpose of the reconciliation of creation took place "in the Son" (1:19–20); and finally, in this way all of reality has its meaningful coherence "in the Son" (1:17).

Head of the Church (Colossians 1:18a)

Paul's balanced middle stanza now concludes by introducing Christ's relationship to his redeemed people, the church. This serves to prepare the reader for the third stanza, which celebrates the Son's work of reconciliation (Col. 1:18b–20). Within the context of the poem, this line is almost shocking in effect. The language of the church as the body of Christ is so familiar to us that we tend to miss the impact of this poetic shift in focus. Paul has been speaking in rather cosmic terms of the Son as the image of the invisible God, the heir of creation, the agent who made the whole universe, the one with priority over all, and the very sustaining center of existence. When the last line of the middle stanza says that the Son is also the head, one might not quite anticipate what is to follow. Elsewhere Paul says that Christ is the head of all rule and authority (Col. 2:10). But here something unexpected follows.

The Son is the head of "the body." Suddenly we are on very earthly ground. What is this body? One must use some sanctified imagination. This little group of gathered believers at Colossae, rejected and despised by the wider religious community, listens to the reading of the poem. God's Son is the head of the body— and the body is the church! The impact had to be exhilarating. Here is where the fellowship of believers in Christ fit into God's grand purpose. "The body" is again identified in Colossians 1:24, in the context of Paul's sufferings, as "[Christ's] body, that is, the church." What a response to the opposition who would pass judgment on and disqualify the believers (2:16–18)! It is the opposition that is "not holding fast to the Head, from whom the whole body,

99

nourished and knit together . . . , grows with a growth that is from God" (2:19). The opposition may be interested in angelic worship, but Christ, the head of the church, is also the head over all powers (2:10). Paul develops the doctrine of the church on the basis of this Christology more fully in Ephesians, but the implications for the Colossians are powerful.

The metaphor of the "head" should not be reduced to a single literal sense such as "source," "authority," or "unity." It encompasses all these meanings and more; that is the value of the metaphor, and the reason why Paul uses it. Christ, as the head of the body, is the church's unifying source and authority. It is a way of speaking about what it means to be "in Christ" and what it means, with special reference to the church, that "in him all things hold together" (1:17). Rather than drawing out the implications of this metaphor, the apostle uses it to introduce the final stanza of his poem and the theme of Christ's reconciling work.

God's Son as Reconciler (Part 3, Colossians 1:18b–20)

Beginning of the New Creation (Colossians 1:18)

"He is the beginning" matches the opening line of the poem, "He is the image of the invisible God" (Col. 1:15), and introduces the third part of Paul's poem. In that first stanza, the primary focus was on the original creation, and the Son's relationship to it, rooted in his identity as the Father's image. Here, the primary focus is on the Son's redemptive work, which has just been thematically introduced by the last line of the middle stanza: he is the head of the body, the church. So when Christ is described here as "the beginning," the reference is not to the beginning of creation, but the beginning of the new creation.[23] The term "beginning" echoes the opening line of the Bible: "In the beginning God created" (Gen. 1:1). This suggests that we are to think also of Christ's reconciling work as a creation, a new creation (2 Cor. 5:17–19). This focus on

23. This is Calvin's view, according to O'Brien, *Colossians*, 50.

the Son's redemptive work is confirmed by the next line, where Christ will be described as "the firstborn from the dead."

Firstborn of the Resurrection (Colossians 1:18)

"The firstborn from the dead" continues the parallelism and matches the second line of the first stanza, "the firstborn of all creation" (Col. 1:15). The meaning is not that the Son was the first to rise from the dead, any more than the Son, as "firstborn of all creation," was the first one to be created. Rather, as the "firstborn," the Son has supreme authority over death. His resurrection is the beginning of the new creation; the incarnate Son of God defeats death and rises up as Lord of all. As Paul moves to his practical instructions in Colossians 3, he challenges the believers: "If then you have been raised with Christ, seek the things that are above, where Christ is, seated at the right hand of God" (3:1).

Preeminent One in Both Creation and Re-creation (Colossians 1:18)

The expected parallel line in the second stanza is slightly delayed, as Paul pauses to tie together the supremacy of Christ in both creation and new creation. Christ is firstborn over both creation and the resurrection, "that in everything he might be preeminent" (Col. 1:18). This comprehensive sovereignty was foreshadowed in the central line of the poem, "in him all things hold together" (1:17), and is now made explicit.

Incarnation of the Divine Nature (Colossians 1:19)

The rationale for this total supremacy is now given, as Paul moves to the heart of the gospel. This follows the pattern of the first stanza, where the third line gave the rationale for the Son's inheritance rights over creation ("For in him all things were created" [Col. 1:16]). Here we have the Son, by whom all things were created, entering the created order as the incarnate one: "in him all the fullness of God was pleased to dwell" (1:19). The gospel elements found in the concentrated words of this third stanza

101

include the incarnation, the work on the cross, the resurrection, the reconciliation of the world, and the lordship of Christ.

That Paul is thinking here of the incarnation of deity is made clear later when the apostle writes, "For in him the whole fullness of deity dwells bodily" (Col. 2:9). This doctrine is clearly taught in John 1:1–18 and Hebrews 1:1–4; it was implicit in Paul's earlier writings (Rom. 8:3; 2 Cor. 8:9; Gal. 4:4–5). The subject of the poem is emphatically God the Son. Paul refers to "the fullness [of God]" (Col. 1:19) and "the whole fullness of deity" in such a way that focus does not shift away to God the Father.[24] The confession is emphatically about what is happening in the Son. This does not diminish the glory of the Father in any way; Paul's purpose in this context is to celebrate the divine status and function of the incarnate Son.[25]

Reconciler of All Creation (Colossians 1:20)

The apostle now rounds off his poem with a double reference to the reconciling work of the Son. In this way he ends with a final amplification of "all things," to comprehensively include everything "whether on earth or in heaven." The reconciliation includes forgiveness of sins, which relates to the Colossians personally, but also encompasses the broader reconciliation of the universe. In other words, the reference to things whether on earth or in heaven is intended to show the Son's lordship over all as a part of the divine purpose. We find a parallel to this in Philippians 2:9–11, where God exalts Christ so that every knee will bow at this name "in heaven and on earth and under the earth, and every tongue confess that Jesus Christ is Lord, to the glory of God the Father."

Peacemaker (Colossians 1:20)

24. In Colossians 1:19, the Greek has simply "the fullness," and translators rightly on the basis of the term, the context, and the parallel in Colossians 2:9 add the clarifying phrase "of God."

25. Gordon D. Fee, *Pauline Christology: An Exegetical-Theological Study* (Peabody, MA: Hendrickson, 2008), 312.

In the first stanza between the double reference to creation, Paul explained the comprehensive nature of the Son's creative work. It included all things in heaven and on earth, visible and invisible, whether thrones or dominions or rulers or authorities (Col. 1:16). Now, in the final stanza, the apostle explains the means by which Christ's reconciling work, equally cosmic in scope, is accomplished. The incarnate and resurrected Son has made "peace by the blood of the cross" (1:20). Much like the line at the center, which introduced Christ as the head "of the body, the church," so this line must have gripped the hearts of the Colossians. The cosmic Lord, the head of their own community, had reconciled the entire creation by his death on the cross.

When we turn to Philippians 2 in our next chapter, we will find at the center of that confession the proclamation that Christ, on the way to his universal exaltation, became obedient to the point of death, "even death on a cross" (Phil. 2:8). This was what the Colossians had confessed. They were now reconciled "in his body of flesh by his death" (Col. 1:21–23). The gospel, the cosmic sovereignty of the Son, and the final reconciliation of the world cannot be separated from Christ's work on the cross. In 1 Corinthians, we saw that "Christ crucified" was the focus of God's wisdom (1 Cor. 1:18–25). Here we see that this wisdom means the reconciliation of all things; it is how God makes peace. We should not domesticate this. We should not reduce the gospel to individual reconciliation with God, although it surely and wonderfully includes this. The whole universe is at stake! What is astounding is that this Christ-centered wisdom that brings about God's cosmic purposes takes place through the church, which is his body and over which he is the head. This has important practical implications for the Christian community.

Summary and Application of the Wisdom in Christ

Jesus, God's Son and Messiah, is the full revelation of the invisible God. Furthermore, as the agent of creation, he has first place over the entire created order. As the universe's sustaining center, he is also the ruler of the redeemed creation, now manifested in the church. As the preexistent one, and through the incarnation, he embodied the "fullness" of deity and accomplishes the reconciliation of all things. He does this by making peace through his sacrificial death on the cross. It is in this supreme person, and in this comprehensive reconciliation, that the Colossians have come to participate. This is wisdom: the Son as the revealer of God, the sustaining Creator and center of the universe, and the Redeemer who brings redemption and peace. On the basis of this Christology, Paul seeks to maintain the loyalty of the community to the gospel, and lead the people toward maturity in Christ. This works out in practical ways for the Colossians on at least three fronts, which are also directly relevant to our context.

Wisdom in Christ and Perseverance

Paul's primary application of his Christological poem is to the struggling faith of the Colossian believers. This is a classic example of how the New Testament writers apply Christology to the life and needs of the church. In the paragraph leading up to his praise of Christ, Paul prays first that the saints might experientially know God's will "in all spiritual wisdom and understanding" (Col. 1:9). In this way they will grow and be fruitful. Paul then prays that the Christian community will be strengthened by God's power in Christ, so as to persevere with joy and thanksgiving (Col. 1:11–12).[26]

Immediately after Paul's poem, the apostle explicitly applies the message of Christ's cosmic reconciliation directly to the Colossian saints. He reminds the Colossians that they were once alienated, but are now reconciled through Christ's incarnation and death (1:21–22a). Their hope is one day to be presented faultless

26. Paul's prayer for both wisdom and power in the life of the Colossian believers echoes his confession in 1 Corinthians that Christ is the wisdom of God and the power of God (1 Cor. 1:21).

104

before him, if they "continue in the faith, stable and steadfast, not shifting from the hope of the gospel" (1:23).

The wisdom of God in Christ is being proclaimed—in keeping with its cosmic nature—"in all creation under heaven" (Col. 1:23). The new creation of Christ's kingdom begins at the personal level when one responds to Jesus' invitation to the promised eschatological salvation: "Come to me, all who labor and are heavy laden, and I will give you rest" (Matt. 11:28). Paul explains this re-creation explicitly in 2 Corinthians: "if anyone is in Christ, he is a new creation. The old has passed away; behold, the new has come" (2 Cor. 5:17). This happens, the apostle explains, because God in Christ is reconciling the world to himself. Paul continues, "We implore you on behalf of Christ, be reconciled to God" (2 Cor. 5:20). Once a person is reconciled to God, he or she becomes a part of the body, the church, over which Christ is the head. We are then to continue as participants, through an obedient and persevering faith, in God's larger purposes of reconciliation in the world.

Wisdom in Christ and Victory over Opposition

Throughout our study we have found the wisdom of God revealed in a context of rejection and opposition. This is certainly true for the saints at Colossae. By placing God's work in its cosmic context, the apostle assures the struggling Christian community of Christ's absolute sovereignty and ultimate victory. This works out in two particular ways in Colossians: with reference to the false teachers and with reference to the "powers and authorities."

Human Opposition. Paul's rich Christology not only gave the antidote to the misguided teaching of the church's opponents at Colossae, but also encouraged the saints in a culture that was deeply shaped by honor and shame. The followers of Christ felt the ridicule of being openly judged by their opponents (Col. 2:16), with their religious philosophy (2:8) and appearance of wisdom (2:23). The believers felt the social sting of being "disqualified" (2:18). The opponents, with their "plausible words" (2:4) and "human traditions" (2:8), with their publicly visible ascetic practices and rituals (2:16–17), and with their proud claims to secret knowledge of angelic worship, were shaming the Christians. Those who have taken seriously the call of the gospel, with its counterintuitive and countercultural wisdom, should expect opposition from the religious elite and worldly-wise. But how does the Christian deal with the sense of belittlement, the sense of shame?

Paul points to Christ, the Son of God, shamed on the cross, but now highly exalted and the ruler of all.[27] In him believers have found reconciliation and forgiveness, and as a result of the shameful cross Christ will one day present them "holy and blameless and above reproach before him" (Col. 1:22). The church is not destined for shame, but for full enjoyment of "the riches of the glory of this mystery, which is Christ in you, the hope of glory" (1:27). This is why Paul teaches and warns everyone with "all wisdom," so that he can present them complete in Christ (1:28). The opposition would shame them, but Paul struggles for them, "that their hearts may be encouraged, being knit together in love, to reach all the riches of full assurance of understanding and the knowledge of God's mystery, which is Christ, in whom are hidden all the treasures of wisdom and knowledge" (2:2–3). Paul prayed that the believers—already participants in the impending kingdom of God's beloved Son, yet in the midst of opposition and shame—can endure, be patient, have joy, and live a thankful life (1:11–12).

Supernatural Powers. There is an even more insidious opposition that lurks in the background, not only behind the Colossian problem but also behind problems the church faces today. More threatening than human opposition is the reality of opposing higher powers. The precise identification of these powers is part of the difficulty of solving the so-called Colossian heresy. When Paul explicitly addressed the nature of the opposition (Col. 2), he did not directly explain how such powers figure in the false teaching; perhaps there was a connection with the interest in angelic worship (2:18).

27. We will see this more explicitly in our next chapter, on Philippians 2.

Twice in the context of addressing the Colossian opposition, Paul mentions rulers and authorities. On both occasions he seems to be applying the theology of the Colossian poem to the supremacy of Christ over spiritual powers: Christ is the head of all rule and authority (Col. 2:9–10), and God through the Son's crucifixion "disarmed the rulers and authorities and put them to open shame, by triumphing over them in him" (2:15).[28] There may well have been at Colossae a fear of supernatural powers, from which the people thought they could not free themselves without religious ritual and angelic intercession.

Paul's answer is overwhelming: Christ is the sovereign Creator and ruler of all powers (Col. 1:16), and through his work on the cross has decisively defeated any who might oppose God's kingdom (2:15). The cosmic reconciliation that happens in Christ, the peace that he makes through the blood of the cross (1:20), defeats the "domain of darkness" (1:13). As the poem ends, his victory encompasses "all things, whether on earth or in heaven" (1:20). The claims of the opposition are silenced—fear of the evil powers, dependence on religious and ascetic practices, and interest in the worship of the angelic realm are all swallowed up in the triumph of Christ.

This is our triumph as well. Whatever fears we may have, whatever powers grip our individual or collective lives, God's beloved Son both sustains us now and assures us of ultimate victory. Our conflict with powers greater than us may take a different shape from the conflict at Colossae. But whatever forces may be arrayed against us, or the church, are decisively defeated in Christ—the wisdom of God *and* the power of God (1 Cor. 1:25).

As with the rest of the New Testament, there is a balance and tension in Colossians between what we can now know of the Son's victorious reign in our lives and the promised manifestation of his

28. Paul refers to the false teaching as both according to human traditions and "according to the elemental spirits of the world" (Col. 2:8), which could be translated as "according to elementary principles." This expression occurs later in the chapter and seems to relate to religious rules (Col. 2:20). When Paul uses the phrase in Galatians, it also is in a context of external religious rules and regulations (Gal. 4:9–10). So the expression may not be a reference to supernatural powers.

final and complete reign. Through his work on the cross, we are already delivered from the domain of darkness and transferred into his kingdom (Col. 1:13). Through the Son's incarnation and our union with him by faith, we "have been filled in him, who is the head of all rule and authority" (2:10). Through the gospel we are "raised with him through faith" (2:12) and "made alive together with him" (2:13), the very one in whom God has "disarmed the rulers and authorities" (2:15). Since we have identified with him in his death (2:20) and resurrection (3:1), we can now "walk in him . . . abounding in thanksgiving" (2:6), for our life is "hidden with Christ in God" (3:3). Yet we await the final consummation: "when [the Son] delivers the kingdom to God the Father after destroying every rule and every authority and power" (1 Cor. 15:24; cf. vv. 25–28). At that time Christ, who is our life, will appear, and we "will appear with him in glory" (Col. 3:4).

This resurrected life that is hidden with Christ in God and that awaits the final victory is not otherworldly. The wisdom of God in Christ relates to our earthly everyday lives as children of the Son's kingdom. The confession of Christ in 1 Corinthians 8:6 was set in the context of the daily struggles of the Christian community. Likewise, the heightened Christological poem of Colossians touches down in the nitty-gritty of life for the Colossians. This can be seen in the way Paul applies the message of reconciliation to the common life of the church.

Wisdom in Christ and Reconciliation in the World

The gospel brings reconciliation, so that individual believers find peace with God. The gospel also brings reconciliation at the cosmic level, so that opposing powers are finally subjugated. But there is another dimension that should not be overlooked: the wisdom of the gospel brings reconciliation at the social level. Here is wisdom so desperately needed in the church and in our world today. The power of God's wisdom in Christ to bring social reconciliation is illustrated in two ways in Paul's ministry.

First, the wisdom of the gospel brought reconciliation between Jews and Gentiles in Christ's one body, the church. It is only in Christ, as the Christological poem confesses, that "all things hold together." With regard to God's work of re-creation and reconciliation, Christ's work is in and through the church, over which he is the head (Col. 1:17–18). The conflict between Jews and Gentiles at Colossae was a result of the "heresy" that denied the gospel (2:8). Only Christ can bring Jews and Gentiles together; he is the unifying head (2:19).

Social reconciliation is an entailment of the wisdom of God at work in the church. It has immediate application to the Jew-Gentile problem, and Paul develops this at length in his Epistle to the Ephesians, written at about the same time as Colossians.[29] The blood of the cross shed by the incarnate Son of God, which makes peace and brings reconciliation (Col. 1:20), is explicitly applied in Ephesians to the division and hostility between Jews and Gentiles:

> But now in Christ Jesus you who once were far off have been brought near by the blood of Christ. For he himself is our peace, who has made us both one and has broken down in his flesh the dividing wall of hostility by abolishing the law of commandments expressed in ordinances, that he might create in himself one new man in place of the two, so making peace, and might reconcile us both to God in one body through the cross, thereby killing the hostility. (Eph. 2:13–16)

Problems of social reconciliation, especially at the racial and ethnic level, are always complex and difficult. This is certainly true of the hostility between the first-century Jews and Gentiles. The Old Testament law itself, at one level, called for separation. But a proper understanding of God's wisdom in Christ, the mystery of what was hidden in the Old Testament from full understanding but now fully revealed in Christ, is "that the Gentiles are fellow heirs, members of the same body, and

29. See especially Eph. 2:11–3:6.

partakers of the promise in Christ Jesus through the gospel" (Eph. 3:6). It is our common reconciliation to God in Christ that is the basis for reconciliation with one another. This is paradigmatic for social and racial reconciliation in the church. If the Jews and Gentiles are reconciled in one body in Christ, how much more Gentiles and Gentiles! When the church lives this out, an important component of "the manifold wisdom of God" is made known, "even to the rulers and authorities in the heavenly places" (Eph. 3:10). A compelling contemporary application of this wisdom has been among Christians from African communities that were once involved in tribal genocide and are now reconciled in Christ.[30]

A second illustration of social reconciliation, easy to overlook but deeply embedded in Colossians and made explicit in a companion letter, Philemon, is the problem of reconciliation and the institution of slavery. As Paul was penning his Epistle to the Colossians, with its Christological poem in chapter 1, it is not hard to imagine Onesimus, the runaway slave, sitting at his side (Col. 4:7–9). Along with reconciliation of individuals to God, the cosmic powers at the feet of Christ, and ethnic groups to one another, the apostle was perhaps thinking about reconciliation of the slave Onesimus to his master Philemon.

Paul treats various social relationships in chapter 3 (Col. 3:18–4:1), and about half of the verses address slavery (3:22–4:1). In the parallel passage in Ephesians, only about a quarter of the verses relate to slavery.[31] The reason for this special attention, as Doug Moo writes, is that "this letter is being sent along with Onesimus, a slave who is returning to be reconciled (Paul strongly hopes) with his master, Philemon."[32] When Colossians is read among the believers who meet at Philemon's house, the letter to Philemon will also be read (Philem. 2). Both Philemon the master and Onesimus the slave will be present for the readings.[33]

---

30. See the accounts at http://alarm-inc.org/.
31. Moo has an excellent treatment of the slavery question in *The Letter to the Colossians and to Philemon*, especially 292–98 and 369–78.
32. Ibid., 298.
33. See Fee, *Pauline Christology*, 329–30.

What is read in Colossians will inform what is read in Philemon. Together these letters constitute God's wisdom in Christ applied to the case of two men who need to be reconciled—a case complicated by social roles defined by the status quo of the institution of slavery.

While this is not the place for an extended treatment of how the gospel impacts the evil of human slavery, several important points will illustrate how God's wisdom in Christ transforms relationships. First, in keeping with Paul's praise of Christ (Col. 1:15–20), all believers have one Lord.[34] Every social relationship is redefined in light of the truth that Christ is the head of the body, the church. So masters have to treat their slaves "justly and fairly"; they also have a Master in heaven (4:1). This does not mean that Paul is sanctioning slavery. He is rather addressing how Christians at that time, caught in the systems of this world, were to treat one another in light of the wisdom of Christ. The theological seeds for the abolition of slavery are here.[35]

This is confirmed by another important point: in Christ, believers are united in one common body, the church. This is the community or common fellowship over which Christ is the head. As a result, there is "not Greek and Jew, circumcised and uncircumcised, barbarian, Scythian, slave, free; but Christ is all and in all" (Col. 3:11). Paul tells the Galatians the same thing: since they have put on Christ, "there is . . . neither slave, nor free . . . You are all one in Christ Jesus" (Gal. 3:28). This common life changes the way we treat each other. Paul prays at the beginning of his letter to Philemon that "the [fellowship or common life] of your faith may become effective for the full knowledge of every good thing that is in us for the sake of Christ" (Philem. 6).[36] Paul is praying that this slave master will have sufficient Christian wisdom with regard to the church's common life in Christ to do the right thing

34. In the nine verses on social relationships, Colossians 3:18–4:1, the lordship of Christ is mentioned seven times.

35. See Moo, *The Letters to the Colossians and to Philemon*, 377 and especially n44.

36. While the ESV translates the word here as "sharing," it is the Greek word *koinonia*, which is used throughout the New Testament for one of the essential marks of the church: the communion of saints.

111

with regard to Onesimus. The goal is that Philemon might have Onesimus back "no longer as a slave but more than a slave, as a beloved brother" (Philem. 16). Paul instructs Philemon, as the apostle's "partner" in the gospel, to welcome Onesimus—not as a slave, but as if he were the apostle himself (Philem. 17). Here is true reconciliation, based on the wisdom of God in Christ.

It is the reconciliation based on the self-sacrificing work of Christ on our behalf that provides a pattern for our social relationships. As the "image of the invisible God" (Col. 1:15), Christ teaches us, as the second Adam, how to live as humans and how to be reconciled to one another. With regard to Onesimus and Philemon, Paul does not explain this with words; he models it by his actions. In Colossians, Paul taught that slaves who were wrongdoers would be paid back for the wrong they had done (3:25). But when he writes to the slave master, he takes this debt on himself: "If he has wronged you at all, or owes you anything, charge that to my account. . . . I will repay it" (Philem. 18–19). Through the wisdom of the gospel, we too can work for and find reconciliation among the broken relationships of this life: recognizing that we have one Lord, that we are one body in him, and that he has taught us to sacrifice our own rights to bring about such reconciliation.

Christian wisdom moves from the heights of Christology to the flesh and blood of our common life. We saw this in 1 Corinthians, where the confession of Christ (1 Cor. 8:6) was made in the context of giving up our own rights out of concern for our brothers and sisters for whom Christ died (1 Cor. 8:7–13). We have seen this in Colossians, where the poem of praise to Christ (Col. 1:15–20) has had immediate practical application to reconciliation in the life of the church. This practical nature of the wisdom of the gospel will become central in our next Christological text.

Wisdom and the Way of the Cross (Philippians 2:5–11)

Have this mind among yourselves, which is yours in Christ Jesus, who, though he was in the form of God, did not count equality with God a thing to be grasped, but made himself nothing, taking the form of a servant, being born in the likeness of men. And being found in human form, he humbled himself by becoming obedient to the point of death, even death on a cross. Therefore God has highly exalted him and bestowed on him the name that is above every name, so that at the name of Jesus every knee should bow, in heaven and on earth and under the earth, and every tongue confess that Jesus Christ is Lord, to the glory of God the Father.

Introduction

What shapes the way we live? What cultural practices and patterns of thinking have made us who we are? These are important questions. We must be thoughtful and intentional here; otherwise, by default, we capitulate to the ways of the world. Christ calls us to be shaped by the way of the cross. But what exactly does this look like? Our study of God's wisdom in Christ comes now to one of the most significant passages in all of Paul's writings. It paints a beautiful and yet immediately practical picture of the life to which Christ calls us.

113

A little over a decade ago, Ralph Martin wrote that Philippians 2:6–11 had not yet yielded its full secrets.[1] A recent book argues that this passage is Paul's "master story," and reveals much about Paul's Christology and his doctrine of God.[2] If a writer of the New Testament applied the wisdom of Christ directly to the life and mission of the church, what would it look like? Philippians 2 provides a wonderful example.

It is easy to overlook the fact that Paul is appealing here to Christian wisdom. Sometimes a word-study approach to Scripture can restrict our focus and cause us to miss important connections. While Paul does not use the common word for "wisdom" (*sophia*) in Philippians, he is addressing the subject in a most profound manner. A word closely related to "wisdom" is "insight" (*phronēsis*).[3] This word and its cognates (or lexically related words) are important in Philippians. The connection between this word set and wisdom is illustrated in the saying of Jesus: "Everyone then who hears these words of mine and does them will be like a wise man (*phronimos*) who built his house on the rock" (Matt. 7:24). Here the word for "wise" is not *sophos* but *phronimos*. Paul sets these two words in parallel in Ephesians 1:8 when he reminds believers that the mystery of God's will, the gospel of Christ, has been made known to them "in all wisdom (*sophia*) and insight (*phronēsis*)."

Paul repeats various forms of this word in the verses leading up to Philippians 2:6–11. Notice the words in italics:

> So if there is any encouragement in Christ, any comfort from love, any participation in the Spirit, any affection and sympathy, complete my joy by *being of the same mind* [*phronēte*], having the same love, *being* in full accord and *of one mind* [*phronountes*]. Do nothing from rivalry or conceit, but in humility count others more significant than yourselves. Let each of you look not only to his

---

1. Ralph P. Martin and Brian J. Dodd, *Where Christology Began: Essays on Philippians 2*, 1st ed. (Louisville: Westminster John Knox Press, 1998), 169.

2. Michael J. Gorman, *Inhabiting the Cruciform God: Kenosis, Justification, and Theosis in Paul's Narrative Soteriology* (Grand Rapids: Eerdmans, 2009), 194.

3. See the introduction to this book for a discussion of Aristotle's use of this word group.

own interests, but also to the interests of others. *Have this mind* [*phronēte*] among yourselves, which is yours in Christ Jesus.

To have this "mind" as followers of Jesus is a call to a certain "way of life."[4] This "way of life" is the path of wisdom found in Christ and the gospel. It is a call to live with the mind of Christ (1 Cor. 2:16), who is the wisdom of God (1 Cor. 1:24, 30). Applying this wisdom to our personal and communal life, in the power of God's Spirit, is what it means to live in obedience and to "work out [our] salvation with fear and trembling" (Phil. 2:12–13).

We will begin our study with a closer look at Philippians 2:1–4. This will show how Philippians 2:5–11 grows out of the church's collective life, which is critical for a proper understanding of Christian wisdom. Then we will briefly consider the structure of these verses that "almost baffle analysis."[5] Next we will focus on the theological content, which leads us to the cross-centered shape of Christian wisdom and its path to exaltation. We will also see how this wisdom is modeled for the Philippians and for us by Paul and his coworkers.

- The Philippian Community: Wisdom, Worship, and Music
- The Centrality of the Cross and the Structure of Philippians 2:6–11
- Christ's Preexistence: A Surprising Glimpse into the Divine Life (Philippians 2:6)
- Christ's Humiliation: The Path of Divine Wisdom (Philippians 2:7–8)
- Christ's Exaltation: The Great Reversal (Philippians 2:9–11)
- Wisdom Modeled and Applied

The Philippian Community: Wisdom, Worship, and Music

We began our study in a scene where Jesus was teaching and inviting people to be disciples in his school of wisdom (Matt. 11).

4. Ralph P. Martin suggests "way of life" as a translation for "have this mind"; see "The Christology of the Prison Epistles," in *Contours of Christology in the New Testament*, ed. Richard N. Longenecker (Grand Rapids: Eerdmans, 2005), 195.
5. Ibid.

Now, nearly thirty years later, with the church spreading through-out the ancient world, we find ourselves in the midst of a Christian community in Greece. In the context of a privileged Roman colony, where people celebrate their status as citizens, the church at Philippi has a calling to live out God's alternative wisdom in Christ.[6] Paul's instructions echo Jesus' invitation (Matt. 11). The apostle exhorts the church to learn from her Lord and imitate the manner of life that he exhibited in the world.

Paul strategically inserts in his composition a confession that would likely have reminded the Philippians of how they worshiped Christ (Phil. 2:6–11). It is as though the curtain were drawn back on a first-century gathering at Philippi; we hear the community singing, confessing Christ as Lord, and celebrating the gospel.

Even the corporate music of the early church proclaimed God's wisdom in Christ and helped shape its life. While there is much we do not know about early Christian worship and hymnody, certain significant facts are clear. First, we know that during worship the New Testament churches customarily sang "psalms and hymns and spiritual songs" (Col. 3:16; Eph. 5:19).

Second, worship and its music were closely associated with Christ's presence, as well as with the meaning and practice of the Lord's Table. The memory of Jesus singing psalms with his disciples at the Last Supper was still fresh (Matt. 26:30; Mark 14:26). Did the early church imagine the crucified and resurrected Christ singing with them in their communal gatherings? This is suggested by the Epistle to the Hebrews. After Jesus had been perfected through suffering, the words of Psalm 22 are found on his lips: "I will tell of your name to my brothers; in the midst of the congregation I will sing your praise" (Heb. 2:12). Christ is uniquely present by his Spirit when the church gathers in worship around the communion table. At such moments believers are filled with

6. For a helpful study of honor and status at Philippi, see Joseph H. Hellerman, *Reconstructing Honor in Roman Philippi: Carmen Christi as Cursus Pudorum* (Cambridge: Cambridge University Press, 2005).

the Spirit of Christ, "speaking to one another with psalms, hymns and songs" (Eph. 5:18–19).

Third, in this music the exalted Christ was worshiped. In Colossians, Paul says that the church sings this music to God (Col. 3:16), while in Ephesians the music is directed to the Lord Jesus (Eph. 5:19); the shift from God the Father to God the Son is natural for the apostle. The Trinitarian nature of this worship is brought out in Ephesians 5:19–20, where songs from the Spirit are used to make music to the Lord Jesus, while giving thanks to God the Father.

Fourth, this worship and its hymnody were understood as integral to the believing community's spiritual formation and as a locus of its wisdom. This is stated explicitly in Colossians: "Let the message of Christ dwell among you richly as you teach and admonish one another with all wisdom through psalms, hymns and songs" (Col. 3:16). In Ephesians, Paul writes, "Be very careful, then, how you live—not as unwise but as *wise* . . . Do not be foolish, but *understand* what the Lord's will is. . . . Be filled with the Spirit. . . . Speak to one another with psalms, hymns and songs" (Eph. 5:15–19 NIV).[7]

Finally, this worship centered on the cross of Christ and the call for believers to live sacrificially for each other and the gospel mission. This practical wisdom was illustrated by the Lord Jesus when he washed his disciples' feet—an act that became another liturgical practice in the early church (John 13:1–17). There are striking parallels between that event of humble service at the Last Supper and the structure of Philippians 2:6–11.[8]

Paul captures this sacrificial service well when he writes in Ephesians 5:1–2—again using liturgical language—"Follow God's example, therefore . . . and walk in the way of love, just as Christ loved us and gave himself up for us as a fragrant offering and sacrifice to God."[9] The theme of the exalted Christ's

7. See the edifying purpose of prayer and music in Paul's instructions on tongues (1 Cor. 14:15–17). Prayer and music are connected in the context of the gathered community in James 5:13.

8. See Gerald F. Hawthorne, *Philippians*, Word Biblical Commentary 43 (Waco, TX: Word, 1983), 78–79.

9. NIV

sacrifice and the church's mission to follow in this path are aptly illustrated in the worship music of Revelation 5:10–11:

> And they sang a new song, saying, "Worthy are you to take the scroll and to open its seals, for you were slain, and by your blood you ransomed people for God from every tribe and language and people and nation, and you have made them a kingdom and priests to our God, and they shall reign on the earth."

In Philippians 2:6–11, we are in touch with this worshiping life of the early church, and much of what we have seen above about worship and its music finds amplification here. Whether the confession was freshly written by Paul or contains preexisting hymnic material, it echoes the songs and praises of the early Christians gathered in worship.

There are interesting historical connections as well. It was at Philippi, in the earliest days of the founding of the community, that we find Paul and Silas in prison suffering for the gospel and *singing* (Acts 16:25). In the darkness of their cell, they were praying and singing "hymns" to God. When the Lord intervened with an earthquake, and the jailer in fear responded to the gospel, the text says that the apostle called on him to "believe in the Lord Jesus." The narrative concludes that "he was filled with joy because he had come to believe in God—he and his whole family" (Acts 16:31–34). The narrative shift from belief in Jesus to belief in God is documented by another historical reference, this time from a secular source. Not too many miles from Philippi, early in the second century, Pliny the Younger, a Roman governor, wrote a letter to the Emperor Trajan about the Christians. He reported that when they gathered, they "chant verses alternately amongst themselves in honor of Christ as if to a God."[10]

A closer look at the literary structure of Philippians 2:6–11 reinforces this sense of being in a place of Christological worship. It also helps to prepare for our consideration of the confession's theological content as it relates to wisdom.

10. *Epistolae*, 10.96; cf. Rev. 5:1–14. See Martin, *Where Christology Began*, 3.

The Centrality of the Cross and the Structure of Philippians 2:6-11

As we saw from our study of Colossians 1:15–20, artistic form and theological content often reinforce one another in these Christological passages. Colossians focuses on Christ as Lord over both creation and salvation. At the center of the literary structure, and serving as a hinge connecting its two major parts, was the expression "in him all things hold together" (Col. 1:17). Here in Philippians, where the pattern for Christian wisdom is "the way of the cross," we find at the pivotal center of the composition the expression "even death on a cross" (Phil. 2:8).

Some critical scholars have suggested that the line "even death on a cross" was inserted by Paul into a preexisting hymn. In their view, it disturbed the nature of the original hymn.[11] However, the layout below suggests that this expression is the deliberately designed axis to the whole. While there can be little doubt that Philippians 2:6–11 reflects the confessional life of the church, and quite possibly the nature of its hymns, the text must be interpreted on its own merit in the context in which the author has set it.

The following layout of the text displays its balanced pattern. There are nine lines leading from the initial line, "he was in the form of God" (Phil. 2:6), to the central line, "death on a cross." Then there are nine lines leading away from the "cross," ending with the climactic "glory of God the Father" (Phil. 2:11).[12] Each section of nine lines can be further divided into three triple-line units, summarizing first the stages of humiliation and then the stages of exaltation.

11. Cf. Peter T. O'Brien, *The Epistle to the Philippians*, New International Greek Testament Commentary (Grand Rapids: Eerdmans, 1991), 230.

12. See Colin Brown, "Ernst Lohmeyer's *Kyrios Jesus*," in Martin and Dodd, *Where Christology Began*, which I follow with some modification. Fee prefers to lay out the poetic structure in two parts, which reflects the two sentences in Greek. Both grammatical form and poetic or artistic lines can be accounted for with the above layout. Scholars continue to debate how best to represent the details; the point here is simply to point out the artistic nature of the composition, and to help us follow its flow.

Three Stages of Humiliation, vv. 6-8

who, though he was in the **form** of God,
did not *count* equality with God
a thing to be exploited,[13]

but *made* himself nothing,
taking the **form** of a servant,
being born in the likeness of **men**.

And being found in **human** form,
he *humbled* himself
by becoming obedient to the point of death,

EVEN DEATH ON A CROSS.

Three Stages of Exaltation, vv. 9-11

Therefore God has highly *exalted* him
and *bestowed* on him **the name**
that is above every name,

so that at **the name** of Jesus
every knee should *bow*,
in heaven and on earth and under the earth,

and **every tongue** *confess*
that Jesus Christ is Lord,
to the glory of God the Father.

With the three verbs in the first half of the hymn (italicized in the graphic display above), the descent to the cross is described: (1) Christ did not "count" equality with God something to be exploited (he exhibits a selfless manner of personal being within the Godhead); (2) he "made" himself nothing (as God he humbles himself, taking on human nature); and finally, (3) he "humbled"

13. "Exploited" captures the idea of the verb here better than "grasped." See NRSV; O'Brien, *Philippians*, 214–16.

himself (in his humanity, he imitates the pattern displayed in his deity). This last point is critical, but often overlooked. It is his self-humiliation and sacrificial love that exhibit a wisdom rooted in God's own life.

Another literary device that holds these first three units together is the repetition of key words (see the words in bold print): unit two picks up the word "form" from the previous unit, and unit three repeats the word "man" from unit two. Christ who was in the "form" of God takes on the "form of a man." Then Christ who has become a "man" humbles himself as a "man" (human) to the point of an obedient death. These three stages of humiliation bring the structure to its pivotal center, and the expression of utter degradation: "even death on a cross."

Now the confession turns upward to exaltation and glory. The second set of three successive units is again tied together by word repetitions (see again the words in bold print). The Son's God-given "name" is mentioned in the first unit, then repeated as the "name" that belongs to Jesus in the second unit. In honor of this name "every knee" bows in unit two, and in the final unit "every tongue" confesses Christ as Lord.

Again, observe the finite verbs (italicized in the graphic display above). In the first unit of this second half, the momentum of the composition seems to gather itself with God's double response to the servant's sacrificial obedience. Here is the only unit of the six that has two finite verbs: God has highly "exalted" him and "bestowed" on him the name. The next two units display the results. In response to the exaltation, every knee will "bow." In response to the bestowal of the name, every tongue will "confess" that name with the climactic declaration, "Jesus Christ is Lord."[14]

14. Some have speculated that the last line ("to the glory of God the Father") may have been sung antiphonally after each part of the hymn. See George Howard, "Phil 2:6–11 and the Human Christ," *Catholic Biblical Quarterly* 40 (1978): 378n30. It is interesting to do this after each of the five other units, along with the last, and also with the central single line "even the death of the cross." While this may simply be a creative improvisation on what Paul himself has written, it shows how this material is amenable to confession and musical celebration.

There are allusions to the Suffering Servant of Isaiah 52–53 in Philippians 2:6–11. At the turning point, we find the humble servant suddenly being exalted by God. Here is wisdom's secret: the call to the way of the cross is the call to the path that leads to the glory of God and to our participation in that glory. In redeeming us from our sin, Jesus also sets this astonishing pattern of wisdom. Isaiah prophesied: "Behold, my servant shall act wisely; he shall be high and lifted up, and shall be exalted" (Isa. 52:13).[15] Based on Christ's example, Paul calls the Philippian church to this path of wisdom.

Paul's confession in Philippians 2:6–11, which celebrates God's wisdom in Christ, exhibits an astonishingly rich theology. Here we can examine it only with special reference to how it informs our understanding of Christian wisdom. The confession's theological content can be organized around Christ's preexistence, his state of humiliation, and his glorification.

Christ's Preexistence: A Surprising Glimpse into the Divine Life (Philippians 2:6)

> who, though he was in the form of God,
> did not count equality with God
> a thing to be exploited

The questions we ask of a text tend to circumscribe the answers we receive. When we focus on one question, we tend to exclude other questions, and consequently other answers. In the history of interpretation, two questions have typically been addressed to Philippians 2:6–11. Is Christ a preexistent divine person? And what happened to Christ's deity when he became incarnate? These are important theological questions. But assuming the Trinity and Christ's preexistence, we might ask a different question: what does this text teach us about God and his wisdom

15. Some prefer to translate Isaiah 52:13 as "my servant will prosper" (NASB) rather than "my servant shall act wisely."

in Christ? When we approach the text with this question, we hear other important and surprising answers.

The evidence from Philippians 2:6–11 for Christ's deity is compelling.[16] The composition begins and ends in the same place—Christ identified with God. At the beginning, the Son is in the form of God, sharing equality with God (2:6); at the end, the Son is confessed as "Lord" (2:11).[17] Through the incarnation, humiliation, and exaltation of Christ, redemption is accomplished and the church is swept up with the Son into participation in the divine purposes for the Father's glory.

Two points are critical to interpreting Paul's Christology. First, along with the other New Testament writers, the apostle assumes Christ's preexistence.[18] However, because this doctrine was confessed early and was widespread in the first-century church, Paul did not explicitly build a case for it. Second, while Paul does not argue for the preexistence of Christ, he regularly builds on the doctrine to make some pastoral or ethical point. This is what we find in Philippians 2. The apostle's primary purpose is not to tell us about the preexistence and deity of Christ. Rather, the apostle wants to teach the church about what God is like, and about what the divine Christ is therefore like, and consequently about what we, as God's redeemed image bearers, should also be like. To clarify this, we need to look at two questions: What does Philippians 2:6 teach us about God? And is Paul presenting Christ in Philippians 2:6–11 as the second Adam?

What Is God Like?

For Paul to say that Christ was "in the form of God" is truly astonishing! Any explanation other than the doctrine of the Son's preexistence and full participation in the Godhead does not

---

16. See the helpful review of all the Philippians material in Fee, *Pauline Christology*, 370–417, and on Philippians 2:6–11, 372–401.

17. We saw the same pattern in John 1:1, 18.

18. The high Christology we saw in Matthew and John is Paul's theology, too. Likewise, the Father's sending of the Son is the same narrative that Paul assumes here (see Rom. 8:3; Gal. 4:4).

adequately account for this phrase in its biblical context. Paul's use of the word "form" by itself does not prove Christ's deity. The word may entail a reference to nature or essence, but this is debated. In this context, "form" seems to emphasize Christ's divine status before the incarnation, just as the expression "form of a servant" emphasizes his status as a slave after the incarnation. This focus on status would be especially significant to the citizens of the Roman colony of Philippi.

The phrase "form of God" may intentionally anticipate the idea of "exaltation" and "glory" at the end of the confession (Phil. 2:11). The point is that Christ has this majestic status, this dress of richness and glory, the very "form" of God. In the context of the hymn, Paul's other teachings, and the entire narrative context of the New Testament, Philippians 2:6 implies Christ's divine preexistence.

That Christ would, nonetheless, have the mind-set not to cling selfishly to his divine equality, but to make himself nothing and exchange the "form" (majestic status) of God for the "form" (humble and impoverished status) of a servant, is doubly astonishing. However, we must not move too quickly to the incarnation. In this first unit of the composition we are in an earlier stage, the eternal preexistence of the Son, where the movement toward the incarnation begins. This is the triple astonishment—that Christ, as the Son of God, as God himself, would exhibit this self-effacement for the sake of others. Here, before he ever takes on human nature, God shows himself in his divine nature to be one who cares sacrificially for others. He does not cling to his rightful glory, but "empties himself" or "makes himself nothing." Here we catch a glimpse into the truly unexpected life of God's servantlike being. Theologically, we are in over our heads. Who can explain such a mystery? Christ, however, is the revealer of God, and here we see Christ shaping our understanding of the character of God. The powerful are typically self-serving and exploiting. But Christ shows God to be self-giving and loving.[19] This way of life leads

19. See Fee, *Pauline Christology*, 383.

God to become a man and to die on a cross. What a supreme astonishment! Here is the wellspring of all wisdom!

We step back from the mystery in silence, for Paul's purpose is not speculative but practical. We are being called to this same way of being in our communal life and for our mission in the world. If we want to know how to live as God's children, as human beings made in his image, we must follow Christ's example.

Adam was made in God's image, and by his disobedience led the human race into sin and rebellion. Christ has rescued us from the fall and taught us how to live faithfully as God's image bearers. This leads to the second question. Is Christ being presented as the second Adam, and if so, in what sense?

How Is Christ Related to Adam?

As with other Christological passages, New Testament scholars have tried to understand Philippians 2:6–11 against various backgrounds.[20] Sometimes such studies shed light; at other times they seem more like rabbit trails. One rabbit trail was the attempt to interpret Paul's composition against the background of a gnostic redeemer myth.[21] Reading it against a Jewish Wisdom figure was also exaggerated and misleading.[22]

A more recent proposal has been that Paul, or the author of an earlier hymn taken up by the apostle, wrote the composition against the background of Adam speculation. The phrase "in the form of God" would arguably remind readers that Adam was made in the "image" or "likeness" of God (Gen. 1:26–27; 5:1). The interpretation goes like this: as God's image bearer, Adam greedily wanted to be like God, but Jesus as the perfect image bearer illustrated humility instead (Phil. 2:6). Adam was disobedient, and this led to death; Jesus was obedient, and this led to a saving

20. These are treated helpfully by O'Brien, *Philippians*, 193–98.
21. This proved to be misguided, not least because the gnostic redeemer myth turned out to be post-New Testament.
22. In Second Temple Jewish literature on the Wisdom figure there is no humility, incarnation, or obedient death. Furthermore, the composite narrative for the Wisdom figure derived from disparate intertestamental literature is suspect.

125

death (2:8). Adam's condemnation is then contrasted with Jesus' exaltation (2:9–10). Finally, Jesus' heavenly glory is compared with Adam's original glory (2:11). While this view is interesting, it breaks down on close analysis.[23] What usually attends this construction is a denial that the text speaks at all of Christ's preexistence: Adam lived in disobedience before God, while Jesus, a better human, lived obediently before God. But this flies in the face of the New Testament's narrative about Christ, and does not adequately explain Philippians 2:6–11. While the gnostic redeemer myth and the account of the Jewish Wisdom figure are likewise mistaken, what made them attractive to scholars was their assumption of preexistence. While the Adam narrative must be rejected as an inadequate framework for the hymn, this does not mean that Christ as the image of God does not suggest an important theological echo with regard to Adam and Adam's race.

The best approach to Christological passages sets them in the context of the commonly received narrative that undergirds the New Testament: the Father sends his preexistent Son into the world as the promised Messiah to reveal God, to redeem his people, and to restore the whole creation. This narrative has as its proper background not only the life and teachings of Jesus, but also the Old Testament Scriptures confessed by Jesus and the earliest church. The claim of Jesus and the apostolic circle was that these things happened "according to the Scriptures." So it should not surprise us to find multiple themes from the Old Testament in the New Testament Christological passages.

So how might the figure of Adam be in the background of Paul's Christological confession in Philippians? There have been two proposals.[24] The first reflects a weak Christology, where a merely human Christ is rewarded by exaltation to God's right hand. This view is rightly rejected. The second view has a high Christology, where Christ is recognized as preexistent. However, this view still sees in the composition an intentional contrast between

23. For a good critique, see N. T. Wright, *The Climax of the Covenant* (Minneapolis: Fortress, 1992), 91–92, 97.

24. See Fee, *Pauline Christology*, 375n16.

Adam's failure and Christ's obedience as the second Adam. Fee rejects both views, arguing that there is a lack of linguistic connection between Philippians 2 and Genesis 2–3.[25]

While this may be true, there is a theological point that even Fee recognizes. Paul presents Christ as the pattern for our life. This Christ was "in the form of God," which is at least to say that Christ is in the "likeness" of God. What Christ models is a fleshing out of the "image of God" in which Adam's race has its fulfillment. As Fee puts it, "Hereby Christ not only reveals the character of God but from the perspective of the present context also reveals what it means for us to be created in God's image, to bear his likeness and have his 'mind-set.'"[26] In this qualified sense, there is an Adam Christology at work here.

Christ's Humiliation: The Path of Divine Wisdom (Philippians 2:7–8)

The Act of Divine Self-Denial

> but made himself nothing,
> taking the form of a servant,
> being born in the likeness of men.

The first question traditionally asked of our text concerns Christ's preexistence. The apostle assumes this doctrine as the basis for his point: the preexistent one provides a pattern of godlikeness for the community precisely in his selflessness. The second question traditionally asked of our text is: What happened to Christ's deity when he became incarnate? Again, the question is important to an orthodox Christology, although it is not the apostle's primary focus.

The great creeds of the church faithfully synthesized the New Testament data on the two natures of Christ within the context of the Trinity. Christ preexisted his earthly life as the eternal Son

25. Ibid., 376, 390–93.
26. Ibid., 388.

127

of God, the second person of the Godhead. At the incarnation, he took on a second nature (his human nature), while remaining one person, now fully God and fully man. How Christ's human and divine natures related to one another during his earthly life is complex, but the distinction and completeness of the two natures along with the unity of his person must be affirmed.[27]

Much ink has been applied to the question of what Paul meant when he said that Christ "made himself nothing" (Phil. 2:7). Did Christ cease to be God? Did he give up some of his divine attributes? The orthodox response has been that Christ did not cease to be God. Instead, what he denied himself was the independent use of his divine attributes, choosing to live in his incarnate state completely obedient to the Father. At times, the second person of the Godhead acted through his human nature (e.g., when we see him sleeping in a boat), and sometimes he acted through his divine nature (e.g., when we see him raising the dead). But during the incarnation, he always acted in submission to the will of the Father. This is how he "made himself nothing."

While this is an important theological discussion, the apostle's focus here is on the "mind" or wisdom that characterized the Son's self-effacement, the next step in the downward path of the incarnation. The journey began with a confession that Christ, in his preexistent life, did not "count" his equality with God "something to be exploited." This was the Son's wise way of being—the way of the unselfish triune life. But now, at the moment of the incarnation, the Son—in response to the missional call of the Father—acted in keeping with that divine character and "made himself nothing." Christ, as the Son of God, is moving in mysterious and divine "self-denial" from his place of glory to serve others.[28] This is Paul's main Christological point.

We should not underestimate this sacrificial mind-set so characteristic of the Son. Nor should we think of it only in terms

27. For a helpful recent study, see Fred Sanders and Klaus Issler, *Jesus in Trinitarian Perspective: An Introductory Christology* (Nashville: B&H Academic, 2007).

28. We put "self-denial" in quotes because in one sense God is not denying himself. The Son of God is acting in full consonance with his divine nature to be oriented to others: by displaying his love, he glorifies himself.

of the exercise of divine attributes. It is not just characteristics such as omnipotence and omniscience that are at stake, but also divine communion. Being in the "form of God" and sharing equality with God involve the preexistent Son's personal communion with the Father. He was "with" the Father, "at the Father's side," sharing his glory (John 1:1, 18; 17:5). It was this, too, that he was willing to sacrifice. There is ineffable mystery here. This divine self-denial is actually a reflection of that life of communion—a life of love oriented toward others. Consider the key words in Philippians 2:1–2 ("encouragement," "comfort," "love," "participation," "affection," "sympathy," "joy," "full accord," "one mind"). These describe, though transcribed for human experience, qualities of the divine life that the Son shared with the Father. This sweet communion, now made available to the church, was included in what Christ was willing to sacrifice. We can but bow in silence.

The Act of Servant Incarnation

Two clauses now explain what the eternal Son of God did when he made himself nothing: he took the form of a servant and was born in the likeness of men. The incarnation is assumed, and is implied by two verbs: the Son of God took another form, and was born with another likeness. This likeness was that of a man, or to put it in Johannine language: the Word became flesh (John 1:14). And this form that he took was that of a servant.

An important component of the New Testament's complex portrait of Jesus is that of a servant who suffered. This picture was informed by Jesus' own self-identification, grounded in the Suffering Servant passages of Isaiah, as well as other Old Testament texts.[29] This connection is made at the beginning of Jesus' public ministry. Luke records:

> Now when all the people were baptized, and when Jesus also had been baptized and was praying, the heavens were opened, and

29. E.g., Pss. 2; 110; Dan. 7; Zech. 9–14. The Servant Songs of Isaiah include Isaiah 41:8–10; 42:1–9, 18–20; 49:1–13; 50:4–11; 52:13–53:12; and 61:1–3.

the Holy Spirit descended on him in bodily form, like a dove; and a voice came from heaven, "You are my beloved Son; with you I am well pleased." (Luke 3:21–22)

The descending of the Spirit and the voice from heaven together identify Jesus as both the promised Messiah and the Suffering Servant. Isaiah had written:

Behold my servant, whom I uphold, my chosen, in whom my soul delights; I have put my Spirit upon him; he will bring forth justice to the nations. (Isa. 42:1)

In the next chapter of Luke, Jesus begins his public ministry. At Nazareth he enters a synagogue and preaches what might be considered his inaugural sermon. He takes an Isaiah scroll and reads from a servant passage:

The Spirit of the Lord is upon me, because he has anointed me to proclaim good news to the poor. He has sent me to proclaim liberty to the captives and recovering of sight to the blind, to set at liberty those who are oppressed, to proclaim the year of the Lord's favor. (Luke 4:18–19, quoting Isa. 61:1–2)

Jesus then rolled up the scroll and sat down. When the eyes of everyone in the synagogue were on him, he proclaimed, "Today this Scripture has been fulfilled in your hearing" (Luke 4:21). Jesus was claiming, "I am the Servant of the Lord!" In one sense the title is honorific; here is God's uniquely anointed servant. But the job description is precisely that of "servant," and the abasement we find in Philippians is the humiliation of the servant that we find in Isaiah.

The best known of the Servant Songs, Isaiah 52:13–53:12, especially informs our text. In this song the title "servant" occurs twice: "Behold, my servant shall act wisely" (52:13) and "By his knowledge shall the righteous one, my servant, make many to be accounted righteous, and he shall bear their iniquities" (53:11).

130

Paul adds to the themes in Isaiah 52:13–53:12 that this movement to a Suffering Servant status originated in the pre-existent divine status of Christ. Our understanding of Isaiah's Suffering Servant passages as background to Philippians should therefore be tempered by several points. While the Suffering Servant texts clearly inform Paul's theology, they are not apart from the redemptive-historical events of the gospel itself. Furthermore, in the person and work of Christ, multiple strands from the Old Testament come together so that no single Old Testament motif can adequately explain the New Testament's confessions about Christ. Finally, the identification of Christ with the Suffering Servant is an inherited assumption under the surface rather than explicitly argued in Philippians 2. Paul's purpose is not to make the connection; this was already part of the early church's understanding of Christ. However, Paul is building on this understanding against the backdrop of Christ's glorious preexistence to make a pastoral point. The apostle's purpose is to call the church to imitate the preexisting Son's unique pattern of living sacrificially for others. Isaiah can now be read from this fuller perspective. It is in this act of divine self-denial that the Lord's servant acted wisely (Isa. 52:13). We are being called to learn from this way of living, to follow in this divine path.

The second clause, "being born in the likeness of men," rounds out the description of Christ's incarnation. What Paul assumes here, in keeping with the Gospels' birth narratives, is what he teaches elsewhere: "when the fullness of time had come, God sent forth his Son, born of woman, born under the law" (Gal. 4:4); and "God has done what the law . . . could not do . . . sending his own Son in the likeness of sinful flesh" (Rom. 8:3). So the Philippian hymn builds on the confession of the divine preexistence and the incarnation of the Son. But the stress in Philippians is on Christ's voluntary movement from his glorious, divine status to the servantlike status of the incarnation. In the context of Philippians, this movement serves as a wisdom pattern for the church to imitate.

There is a distinction between Christ and the believer, an aspect of his humiliation that we cannot now fully reflect. This may account, in part, for why Paul writes "in the *likeness* of men." Elsewhere, Paul qualifies the Son's humanity as "the *likeness* of sinful flesh" (Rom. 8:3); although fully human, Christ was "without sin" (Heb. 4:15). Unlike him, we are marred by the fall and its consequences. But Paul's main reason for stressing "likeness" may be his focus on the question of Christ's lowly status and appearance: the form of a servant, the likeness of men.

The Incarnate Act of Humble Obedience

> And being found in human form,
> he humbled himself
> by becoming obedient to the point of death,

We come now to the composition's third unit in the Son's downward movement. In the first unit, we saw Christ in his preexistent status display a self-denying mind-set about his rightful prerogatives as God. In the second unit, Christ acted in keeping with that divine wisdom by making himself "nothing," and with his incarnation took on a servant status. It is not surprising then that this same divine person, now living on earth with a human nature, would act after that same pattern. This is exactly what we find in the third unit: "and being found in human form, he humbled himself" (Phil. 2:8). Here is the second Adam showing us how to live as human beings in the image of God. First, Christ modeled godlikeness by making himself nothing and assuming the role of a slave. Then he exemplified true humanity by further humbling himself in obedience to the Father. Is it any wonder then that when Jesus invites us to come and learn from him in his school of wisdom, he describes himself as "gentle and lowly in heart" (Matt. 11:29)?

Christ exhibited his humility "by becoming obedient to the point of death" (Phil. 2:8). Isaiah 53:12 reports of the Suffering Servant, "Therefore I will divide him a portion with the many . . . because he poured out his soul to death." That the early church

132

understood Christ's humility leading to the cross in light of Isaiah 53 is illustrated in Philip's explanation as he presents Christ to the Ethiopian eunuch. Philip quotes the Greek translation of Isaiah 53:8, "In his humiliation justice was denied him. Who can describe his generation? For his life is taken away from the earth" (Acts 8:33).

According to the Gospel of John, Jesus understood his incarnation and its mission as an act of humble obedience to the Father: "I have come down from heaven, not to do my own will but the will of him who sent me" (John 6:38). In John this obedience had its supreme hour in Jesus' death (John 12:27), when the obedience was complete and Jesus cried, "It is finished" (John 19:30). Paul elsewhere teaches that Jesus' life and death were in obedience to God (Rom. 5:19; 2 Cor. 5:21; Gal. 1:4; 3:13). The author of Hebrews teaches that Jesus' obedience demonstrates that he is God's Son (Heb. 1:1–4; 5:1–10; 10:5–10).

The apostle is not setting forth Christ's obedience in order to expound its atoning significance (although this is assumed). Rather, he is arguing that Christ's humble and sacrificial obedience is the path of wisdom for the church. It serves to inform the instructions that follow the confession: "Therefore, my beloved, as you have always obeyed, so now, not only as in my presence but much more in my absence, work out your own salvation with fear and trembling" (Phil. 2:12). Christ's obedience to the Father becomes a pattern for our obedience to Christ and the gospel.

We are approaching the dark and yet marvelous center of Paul's celebration of Christ. Paul has just mentioned that the Lord's humble obedience was unto death. He will now take it up with a repetition that functions as the hinge of the composition and takes us to the utter depths of Christ's suffering: "even death on a cross."

The Centrality of the Cross in the Way of Wisdom

The cross is the literary center between the two balanced parts of this apostolic confession, even as the cohesion of all things in Christ was at the center of the Colossian composition (Col. 1:17). Paul frequently refers to "the cross" or "crucifixion" in his epistles as he focuses on different aspects of Jesus' saving death.[30] What is unique in Philippians 2, however, is that the focus is *not* primarily on the benefits of his substitutionary work, *but* on what the cross meant first in Christ's own experience and then as an example for the church at Philippi.

Here is the path Jesus took. In his divine life as the eternal Son of God, he existed with a wisdom that would not exploit privileged status. Instead, he lived in deferential harmony with the Father and the Spirit. In the fullness of time, and in keeping with this triune way of being, he took on through the incarnation the status of a slave. Continuing on his path as the second Adam, Christ now lived in a fashion that fully reflected the image of God by humbling himself in perfect obedience to the Father. In the wonder of God's saving purposes, this obedience led Christ to his death. In what must have seemed incredible to the ancient world, this was "even death on a cross."

Such sacrificial humility would have been unexpected to the citizens of a Roman colony such as Philippi, with their focus on self-aggrandizement and status. The juxtaposition of Christ's status as a slave and the manner of his death combine to strike at the heart of all status-seeking ways of life. Here is the epitome of degradation and suffering! Here, too, are the wisdom and power of God. It is Christ's death on the cross that Paul had identified as the wisdom and power of God (1 Cor. 1:23–24; cf. 1:26–27; 2:1–4). Christ crucified is the counterintuitive reality of divine wisdom and power. This wisdom leads to the saving power of the gospel, but also to a transformed manner of life in the world, one that imitates the "mind of Christ" (1 Cor. 2:16). Philippians illustrates the application of this surprising wisdom in the life of the church. When Christ made himself nothing, took on human nature, and then humbly and obediently went to the cross, he set "the ultimate paradigm for all relationships within the believing

---

30. O'Brien, *Philippians*, 231–32.

community."[31] *The cross is the locus of God's redemptive wisdom in Christ, and the cross is also the wisdom-way for the life of the church.* "Have this mind among yourselves, which is yours in Christ Jesus" (Phil. 2:6).

Christ's Exaltation: The Great Reversal (Philippians 2:9-11)

The second half of the Christological confession, with its balancing three units of three lines each, leads away from the cross to exaltation and glory. It reveals God the Father's exaltation of Christ, vindicating the Son's humble obedience, his cross work, and his path of wisdom. Christ, in whom believers have their mode of life, has become Lord of all. This situates the Christian community both under Christ's exalted reign (for they too bow the knee to his lordship) and also as participants in his exaltation as those who are in Christ. This second part of Paul's composition reveals the narrative's eschatological outcome: the whole universe will one day worship the Son, and every living being will confess his lordship. This defines not only the end of wisdom's path for Christ, but also the end of the journey for the church. This is how the Father will be glorified—and by implication not only Christ, but the church, will participate in this glory.

The Father's Exaltation of the Son (Philippians 2:9)

> Therefore God has highly exalted him
> and bestowed on him the name
> that is above every name,

Paul's composition now shifts from a description of what Christ has done to a joyous declaration of the Father's response to the Son's obedience. This announcement, in the rhetorical context of Philippians, builds on two fundamental convictions of the early church. First, after the Son's sufferings, the Father

---

31. Fee, *Pauline Christology*, 389.

vindicated Jesus both by his resurrection and by his ascension to glory. Jesus asked the two disciples on the road to Emmaus that first Easter morning, "Was it not necessary that the Christ should suffer these things and enter into his glory?" (Luke 24:26).[32] Here again we must read the New Testament narrative against its Old Testament background: "Behold, my servant shall act wisely; he shall be high and lifted up, and shall be exalted" (Isa. 52:13).[33]

The second fundamental conviction was that the Son's pattern of humble suffering followed by glorious exaltation was not only the path for Christ, but also the pattern of wisdom for the church. This was taught as a principle by Jesus: "The greatest among you will be your servant. For whoever exalts himself will be humbled, and whoever humbles himself will be exalted" (Matt. 23:11–12; cf. Luke 14:11; 18:14). Those closest to the Lord repeat his teaching in their epistles: "Humble yourselves before the Lord, and he will lift you up" (James 4:10; see 4:6 and 1 Peter 5:6). The next two units will stress what is unique about Christ in his exaltation, and they will also point the church to her eschatological hope.

The Cosmic Worship of Christ (Philippians 2:10–11)

> so that at the name of Jesus
> every knee should bow,
> in heaven and on earth and under the earth,
>
> and every tongue confess
> that Jesus Christ is Lord,
> to the glory of God the Father.

These final units declare the outcome of the Father's exaltation of the Son. Every living person in the cosmos will bow in honor of Jesus and confess him as Lord. What was rightfully the

32. Cf. Heb. 1:3; 2:9.
33. See also Dan. 7:13–14.

Son's, but that he would not exploit (Phil. 2:6), the Father now confers on him.

The end of Paul's composition is best explained against the backdrop of three factors: the historical reality of Christ's resurrection, ascension, and glorification; the early Christian confession of Jesus as Lord (see Rom. 10:9; 1 Cor. 12:3); and the language of Isaiah 45:23. The use of Isaiah brings us full circle to the starting point of the composition and to the Son's deity (Phil. 2:6); only now Christ is robed in the unique glory gained by his crucifixion—a glory that is for the Father.[34] This pulses with Christological and Trinitarian implications. Much like 1 Corinthians 8:6, where the Son is taken up into the language of the *Shema*, so here Christ is swallowed up, as it were, in the Godhead, by the use of the title "Lord." Isaiah teaches that there is no "Lord" besides God (42:8; 45:6, 18). Yahweh says, "By myself I have sworn, my mouth has uttered in all integrity a word that will not be revoked: Before me every knee will bow; by me every tongue will swear" (Isa. 45:23). This is one of the most radically monotheistic passages in the Old Testament. Yet Paul, without argumentation, applies these words to the Son: every knee bows at Jesus' name, and he is confessed as Lord.[35] Only the deity of the Son within the context of the Trinity can adequately explain how this can be so, and how it can yet be "to the glory of God the Father."[36]

We must be reminded that this early Christian confessional language about Christ comes to us assumed rather than argued, and in the shape of practical instruction to the church. So the question most relevant for our study is how this second half of Paul's celebration of Christ relates to the wisdom of God for his people. How do Christians follow in this path, which turns at the Father's intervention from the way of suffering to that of glory and exaltation?

---

34. Paul teaches in 1 Corinthians 2:7–8 that the hidden and secret wisdom of God involves the crucifixion of "the Lord of glory."

35. We saw this same cosmic supremacy of Christ developed in a different way in Colossians 1:15–20.

36. See Rom. 14:9–12.

Wisdom Modeled and Applied

The answer is found as Paul illustrates this wisdom both by his own life and by that of his companions. The unique "way of thinking," or wisdom, that is presented in Philippians begins in the heart of the triune God; is made incarnate and perfectly embodies itself in the life and cross work of Christ; and then is modeled by Paul and others in the apostolic team. In this sense, the Christological celebration of Philippians 2:5–11 can be said to lie at the heart of the epistle. This wisdom is for the Philippians and for us as well.

Wisdom and the Apostle Paul

Paul taught believers to imitate his life, even as he imitated Christ (1 Cor. 11:1). He taught the Philippians the same thing: "Brothers, join in imitating me" (Phil. 3:17). Paul expects the church at Philippi to read his epistle with this in mind and embeds in his letter examples of Christ's wisdom lived out in his life. These examples illustrate the two parts of the Philippian hymn, exemplifying both humiliation and exaltation.

Humiliation. The letter begins with Paul exemplifying what might be called the Christian's "wisdom status"—that of a servant. Like Christ, Paul takes on the form of a slave (Phil. 2:7). It is only in this epistle that Paul introduces himself as a servant without mentioning his apostleship (1:1). Likewise, it is only in this epistle that Paul, in contrast, addresses the church leaders with their formal titles ("overseers and deacons"). At the outset, the apostle is modeling humility, counting others more significant than himself (2:3). Only the church worker Epaphroditus (2:25) is honored with the title "apostle" ("messenger" [ESV]) in Philippians. By example as well as instruction, Paul models what it means, in self-deference, to honor others (2:29).[37]

37. See J. H. Hellerman, "Brothers and Friends in Philippi: Family Honor in the Roman World and in Paul's Letter to the Philippians," *Biblical Theology Bulletin* 39 (2009): 20–21, 23. In 2 Corinthians 8:23, Paul calls certain Christians who serve the church "apostles" ("messengers" [ESV]) and mentions that such Christians are a glory to Christ.

This nonexploitive way of being, rooted in the nature and life of the triune God, led Christ to "make himself nothing" (2:7). This is the way of wisdom, and the apostle follows in its school. In Philippians 3:4–6, after describing his "status" within Judaism, the apostle cries out that he considered it nothing. Paul could not be more emphatic: "whatever gain I had, I counted as loss . . . I count everything as loss . . . I have suffered the loss of all things and count them as rubbish . . ." (3:7–8). In the context, Paul is surrendering any confidence in the status of the flesh, in order to find righteousness in Christ alone. The mind-set of not clinging to one's status reflects the life of wisdom.

Christ's nonexploitive way of being, and his humility, led to the incarnation and his obedient and purposeful suffering. Here, too, the apostle imitates his teacher in the school of wisdom. Paul, of course, did not become incarnate, but he was willing to remain "in the flesh" for the sake of others (1:22–25). Paul rejoices when Christ is preached, even if that means suffering himself (1:17–18). This was a wisdom principle of Paul's ministry: "I rejoice in my sufferings for your sake, and in my flesh I am filling up what is lacking in Christ's afflictions for the sake of his body, that is, the church" (Col. 1:24). Paul tells the Philippians that he was willing to suffer to the point of death for them (Phil. 2:17). This is what it means to follow the wisdom pattern of Christ.[38] Paul shared all this with his readers to encourage them in their own imitation of Christ: they were not only to believe in Christ, but also to suffer for his sake, joining in Paul's example (Phil. 1:29–30; cf. 1 Peter 2:21). This leads up to Paul's Christological confession in Philippians 2.

Exaltation. Paul intended for the second half of his composition (Phil. 2:9–11) to apply also to the believer's "way of life" or wisdom. This is confirmed by how the apostle illustrates the exaltation theme in his own life. Paul's participation in Christ leads to justification by faith (3:9). In this sense, Christ is Paul's wisdom, even his righteousness (1 Cor. 1:30). But wrapped up in

---

38. See also 1 John 3:16.

his life in Christ is also the anticipation of the glory of the resurrection (Phil. 3:11). For Paul, this meant sharing in the sufferings of Christ and "becoming like him in his death" (3:10). This is the path God's wisdom took for Christ, and Paul imitates it in his own thinking. Paul did not see himself as perfect yet, but pressed on "toward the goal for the prize of the upward call of God in Christ Jesus" (3:12–14). Paul explicitly calls this "way of thinking" (or wisdom) the way of the mature in Christ (3:15).[39] This is why Paul can say: "For me to live is Christ and to die is gain" (1:21).[40]

Wisdom and the Apostolic Team

Paul invites the Philippians not only to imitate him, but also to watch carefully the examples of other faithful believers: "keep your eyes on those who walk according to the example you have in us" (3:17). True followers of Christ live as counterexamples to the "mind-set" (or wisdom) that is oriented to earthly things (3:19).[41] It is the worldly-wise who oppose wisdom's humble obedience and suffering; they live as enemies of the cross (3:18). The worldly-wise seek a different exaltation: they glory in their shame (3:19). This is a reminder that the gospel is set not only in the context of faith, but also in that of rejection.

Paul's pastoral purpose in his Christological confession was to teach the Philippians how to live in the wisdom of Christ, both in their relations with one another and in their life in the world. Wisdom meant to "seek the interest of others," even as Christ did (Phil. 1:4–5). Paul identifies two men from his apostolic band who especially illustrate this pattern of being "others-oriented"— Timothy and Epaphroditus.

39. Paul uses the same word (*phroneō*) here that he used to introduce the Christological confession in 2:1–5.

40. The principle of humility and exaltation, applied to the church in her participation in the way of Christ, is amply attested elsewhere in the New Testament. Peter writes, "Rejoice insofar as you share Christ's sufferings, that you may also rejoice and be glad when his glory is revealed" (1 Peter 4:13; cf. 1 Peter 5:1, 10). Paul elsewhere teaches that we are heirs of Christ, "provided we suffer with him in order that we may also be glorified with him" (Rom. 8:17–18). See Rev. 2:10.

41. Again Paul uses the wisdom word *phroneō*.

The apostle hoped to send Timothy to the Philippians. Paul had trained this young son in the faith about the path of Christlike sacrifice. Paul once wrote to Timothy something the apostle had probably often repeated. It is a type of wisdom saying, and it reflects both parts of Paul's Christological confession in Philippians: "If we have died with him, we will also live with him; if we endure, we will also reign with him" (2 Tim. 2:11–13).

Paul makes it clear that this coworker was not like those who seek their own interests. Timothy was genuinely concerned for the welfare of others (Phil. 2:19–21). The church would recognize Timothy's proven worth, because he had served with Paul in the gospel as a son does with his father (2:22). The Greek word for "serve" here is a verbal cognate of "slave." Timothy wore the robe of wisdom's status: a servant reflecting the likeness of God manifested in Christ. He too had taken on the form of a servant in the way of the cross.

We have already seen how Paul honored Epaphroditus as an "apostle" of the Philippian church. He describes him further as a brother, fellow worker, fellow soldier, and minister to Paul's needs (2:25). Not only had Epaphroditus shown a servant spirit, but he was tenderhearted toward the believers at Philippi. He was especially distressed because they had been concerned over his recent critical illness (2:26). As Christ had lived in humble obedience to the Father "to the point of death" (2:8), so Epaphroditus had "nearly died for the work of Christ" (2:30). The parallel in the Greek is striking: Epaphroditus was "near to the point of death." For his others-oriented suffering in the gospel, this dear Christian, when he arrives at Philippi, is to be honored, and the cause of joy (2:29). This is the wisdom pattern.

The apostle (2:17–18), the apostolic delegate (2:19–22), and the church's own messenger (2:25–29) are presented, in descending order of status, to model the wisdom that the Christological hymn had celebrated. This would have had a powerful psychological impact on the community at Philippi. No matter

141

what one's role in the church, all were to put on the same dress of Christ's humble service.[42]

Wisdom for the Philippians

There is a sense in which the entire Epistle to the Philippians was an application of Christian wisdom. But two particular applications drive home the power of Paul's confession at the heart of the letter. The first application is to the entire community, and captures the significance of the Christological celebration for the church's manner of life. It climaxes with their participation in the glory of Christ's exaltation. The church is called not only to believe in the gospel, but to suffer for Christ (Phil. 1:29). So Paul calls on the community to continue in the humble obedience that Christ modeled (2:12). In this manner, they are to shine as lights in the world, holding forth the word of life (2:15–16). They are to imitate Paul and his coworkers in this path of suffering and to avoid the counter wisdom of the world, which places its confidence in human status and opposes the way of the cross (2:19–3:21).

The outcome of this life of wisdom is a final, glorious participation in the exaltation of Christ (3:20). The Philippians' true citizen status is not in the Roman colony of Philippi. It is in heaven, where Jesus is now enthroned. Living now between humiliation and exaltation, the church awaits her Savior, the Lord Jesus Christ. In a statement filled with linguistic echoes of the hymn in Philippians,[43] the apostle applies the second half of his Christological confession directly to the church: Christ "will transform our lowly body to be like his glorious body, by the power that enables him even to subject all things to himself" (3:21). This is how the journey on the path of wisdom comes to its magnificent end.

The second application relates to a very practical problem at Philippi. There was disagreement between two of the leading women in the church, Euodia and Syntyche. Paul's counsel to

---

42. I thank Robert Peterson, my editor, for the suggestion leading to this paragraph.
43. See O'Brien, *Philippians*, 261.

them at the end of his epistle is profound, yet simple: "agree in the Lord" (Phil. 4:2). We can miss the force of this, unless we see how it recalls Philippians 2, both verbally and conceptually.[44] Paul is applying the exhortation there (2:1–5), with all the rhetorical power of the Christological confession that supports it (2:6–11), directly to them. In effect, Paul challenges them, "Be reconciled in the way of wisdom we have in Christ!" Paul then encourages another believer in the community to help them do this (4:3).

We can envision Euodia and Syntyche weeping and confessing their sins when the letter was read in the congregation. They had been exalting themselves above their Lord by their behavior toward one another. Christ had gone to the cross in self-denying humility for them, but they had mistreated each other in self-importance, failing to look out for the other's interest. Paul's hope was that they would once again worship together, singing hymns to the exalted Christ and celebrating the wisdom of the cross.

Wisdom for Us

To be a disciple in the school of Christ's wisdom shapes not only our thinking, but also our desires and our relationships. When we take on his yoke and learn from him (Matt. 11:29), we begin to participate in God's mission in the world as part of the church. Christ invites us to "rest," but also to suffer.

The life that is ours in Christ Jesus (Phil. 1:5) provides a Trinitarian rest, characterized by "encouragement in Christ" and "participation in the Spirit." This is the Spirit of Christ who has taught us to cry "Abba! Father!" (Gal. 4:6). In this school of wisdom, under the yoke of Christ, our desires are transformed. We experience the "comfort of love" that comes from God, and then begin to practice this same love toward one another, with affection and sympathy, as we strive to live in harmony (Phil. 2:1–3).

Out of this participation in Trinitarian rest and love flows a unique manner of being in the world, one characterized by

44. Again Paul uses the wisdom word *phroneō*.

143

the pattern of the cross. Progress in Christ's school of wisdom calls us to a type of communal life in which we do not exploit our status and power. In humility we live in self-deference, placing the welfare of others above our own (Phil. 2:3–4). It is this sacrificial life for others that is our way of wisdom in Christ. This is not something peripheral to the gospel, a nice moral side benefit to the Christian life; it stems from the heart of the gospel, and the very being of God.

6

Wisdom and the Priesthood of Christ (Hebrews 1:1–4)

Long ago, at many times and in many ways, God spoke to our fathers by the prophets, but in these last days he has spoken to us by his Son, whom he appointed the heir of all things, through whom also he created the world. He is the radiance of the glory of God and the exact imprint of his nature, and he upholds the universe by the word of his power. After making purification for sins, he sat down at the right hand of the Majesty on high, having become as much superior to angels as the name he has inherited is more excellent than theirs.

Introduction

If you have lived the Christian life for very long, you have probably faced "the darkness"—experiences that can feel like "the valley of the shadow of death" (Ps. 23:4). At other times, Christ's call to bear his yoke, although filled with promises of being "easy and light," can seem more like an old burden. There is no "rest," only labor and toil (Matt. 11:28–29). At such times, the New Testament summons us to keep learning from the gentle and lowly Christ.

The community to which Hebrews was written needed such encouragement. Its prologue is an extraordinarily rich

145

announcement of God's amazing wisdom in his Son (Heb. 1:1–4).[1] The author has creatively woven together themes commonly confessed in the early church about Christ, in order to exhort the Hebrews to faithfulness. In this chapter we will see how these themes are used to point to a distinctively Christian view of wisdom, one that can inspire us in our darkest moments to faithfully follow Christ. As with our study of Philippians, we organize our study of this incredibly dense Christological passage around a description of its literary structure.

- The Structure of the Prologue
- The Context of Warning
- Wisdom in Christ, the Ultimate Revelation
- Wisdom in Christ, the Efficacious Redeemer
- Wisdom in Christ, the Supreme Ruler
- Summary of Wisdom in Hebrews

The Structure of the Prologue

The Christological themes and literary structure of Hebrews 1:1–4 signal that we are again on church confessional and perhaps even hymnic terrain. Like the texts we studied in John 1, Colossians 1, and Philippians 2, the prologue to Hebrews is a carefully crafted and dense articulation of the doctrine of Christ.[2] Hebrews 1:1–4 will be displayed graphically and the structure will be briefly explained. It is wonderfully intricate in its symmetry. This structure highlights three New Testament Christological themes around which we will summarize the wisdom of the Son.

---

1. William Lane argues that the author presents Jesus "in the guise of Wisdom" in William Lane, *Hebrews: A Call to Commitment* (Peabody, MA: Hendrickson, 1988), 33. He follows the same reasoning in his commentary, *Hebrews 1–8* (Dallas: Word, 1991), 3–19 and cxxxix. For some concise remarks on this, see Peter O'Brien, *The Letter to the Hebrews* (Grand Rapids: Eerdmans, 2010), 53–54.

2. Other New Testament texts exhibit both this careful literary structure and these common Christological themes: e.g., Eph. 1:3–10; 1 Tim. 3:16. This structural tendency may indicate hymnic features, as well as confessional material.

146

The Text Displayed Graphically

> *Long ago, at many times and in many ways, God spoke to our*
> > *fathers by the prophets,*
> *but in these last days he has spoken to us by his Son,*
> > whom he appointed the heir of all things [Ps. 2:8],
> > > through whom also *he created* [literally "made"] the world.
> > > > **He is the radiance of the glory of God**
> > > > > **and the exact imprint of his nature,**
> > > > **and he upholds the universe**
> > > > > **by the word of his power.**
> > > After *making* purification for sins,
> > he sat down at the right hand of the Majesty on high [Ps. 110:1],
> *having become as much superior to angels*
> *as the name he has inherited is more excellent than theirs.*

The Structure Explained[3]

The key to properly identifying the structure of Hebrews 1:1–4 is in recognizing the description of the Son in his supreme revelatory capacity at the center (bold letters in the graphic display above).[4] Once the center is isolated, the surrounding elements fall into a perfect concentric pattern. At this pivot point, the subject shifts from the Father's speaking in the Son (Heb. 1:1–2) to the Son's own revelatory power (Heb. 1:3).[5] With regard to God, the Son is the radiance of his glory and the exact imprint of his nature; with regard to all else, the Son upholds everything by the word of his power. It is this center that grounds the Son's function as the ultimate revealer of God. Conceptually, the announcement is strikingly similar to John's opening

---

3. This understanding of the prologue's structure is based on an earlier study by the author, which is now summarized in O'Brien, *Hebrews*, 45–46 and n6.

4. For details confirming this feature and other elements of the literary structure, see Daniel Ebert, "Wisdom in New Testament Christology, with Special Reference to Hebrews 1:1–4" (PhD diss., Trinity Evangelical Divinity School, 1998), 12–39.

5. The ESV divides the single Greek sentence into three: the middle sentence reflects the composition's pivotal center.

declaration: "In the beginning was the Word, and the Word was with God, and the Word was God" (John 1:1).

This declaration of the Son's revelatory capacity is thematically balanced by a pair of statements at the beginning (Heb. 1:1–2a) and end (Heb. 1:4) of the prologue (italicized letters in the graphic display above). At these bookends, the Son is displayed as superior to the primary mediators of the Old Testament revelation: prophets and angels.

Immediately around the center are announcements about what has been "made" in relationship to the Son: through him God "made" ("created" [ESV]) the world (Heb. 1:2c); and the Son "made" purification for sin (Heb. 1:3c). The same Greek word is used in both lines.[6] This is intentional and draws the reader's attention to the parallels: the Son is the divine agent of both creation and redemption. We saw these themes similarly balanced in Colossians 1:15–20. Later in his epistle, the author will develop this combination of power and sacrifice in his primary theological contribution—the Son's priesthood.

The remaining lines contain allusions to important Christological psalms, and describe the Son in his messianic or kingly role. The first describes the Son as the appointed heir of all things (Heb. 1:2b). This echoes Psalm 2:8, "Ask of me, and I will make the nations your heritage, and the ends of the earth your possession." The second line describes the Son as seated at the right hand of God (Heb. 1:3d). This echoes Psalm 110:1, "The LORD says to my Lord: 'Sit at my right hand, until I make your enemies your footstool.'"

In this poetic prelude, the author has artistically portrayed the main features of God's wisdom in Christ, resulting in a Christological confession of great rhetorical power. This Scripture-saturated sentence celebrates the triple supremacy of Christ: his comprehensive revelation of God, his powerful work of atonement, and his sovereign cosmic reign.[7] These themes reflect what the

6. The way the second line echoes the first by using the same verb ("made") is often lost in English translations, but see the ASV, the NASB, the New Century Version, and the older Wycliffe New Testament.

7. In the original Greek, the prologue to Hebrews consists of one sentence. This was followed by older English translations (KJV, ASV), although the Wycliffe New Testament

Reformers called the threefold office of Christ: prophet, priest, and king. They also celebrate the main wisdom themes that we have found in our study of New Testament Christology.

The Context of Warning

As we have seen in each of our texts, God's wisdom in Christ elicits both faith and unbelief. Hebrews emphasizes this more than any other book in the New Testament. The epistle is notorious for its warnings, which can have a powerful effect on the conscience.[8] They are not incidental to the author's purpose, but contain the goal of his epistle: to call the church to faithful perseverance in following Jesus.[9]

The five warning sections of Hebrews suggest that to a significant degree, at least, an element of the community was in danger of "falling away."[10] There was a growing breach between the synagogue and the church, with the Christian community becoming an illegitimate religion before the Roman government. The references to prison and the fear of persecution imply that it was not safe to be a Christian.[11] In the midst of disappointment and opposition, there may have been an inclination on the part of these Christians to return to the protection and comfort of Judaism.[12] What could remedy the situation? The author of Hebrews believed that the community had failed to experientially grasp the fullness and effectiveness of God's revelation in his Son; it was, in effect, a failure in the school of Christian wisdom (see especially

---

had two sentences. For stylistic reasons, more recent translations divide it into three (NASB), four (NIV), five (Contemporary English Version), six (NLT, The Message), or even seven (New Century Version) sentences. This tendency reflects the density of the Christological statements.

8. For various approaches, see Herbert W. Bateman, ed., *Four Views on the Warning Passages in Hebrews* (Grand Rapids: Kregel, 2007).

9. Cynthia Westfall vigorously argued this in *A Discourse Analysis of the Letter to the Hebrews: The Relationship between Form and Meaning* (London/New York: T&T Clark, 2005).

10. Heb. 2:1–4; 3:7–4:13; 5:11–6:8; 10:26–39; 12:25–29.

11. Heb. 10:32–35, 39; 12:3; 4:11–12.

12. George Guthrie effectively re-creates a fictitious account of a young man who may well resemble the Hebrews in the situation they were facing; see his *Hebrews* (Grand Rapids: Zondervan, 1998), 17–19.

Heb. 5:11–14).[13] His sermon strongly encourages them to go on
to maturity and warns them of the grave danger of falling away
(Heb. 6:1–6).

The first of these warnings (Heb. 2:1–4) is a direct application
of the prologue (Heb. 1:1–4). The wisdom announced in God's
Son must not be neglected.

> Therefore we must pay much closer attention to what we have
> heard, lest we drift away from it. For since the message declared
> by angels proved to be reliable, and every transgression or dis-
> obedience received a just retribution, how shall we escape if we
> neglect such a great salvation? It was declared at first by the
> Lord, and it was attested to us by those who heard, while God
> also bore witness by signs and wonders and various miracles
> and by gifts of the Holy Spirit distributed according to his will.
> (Heb. 2:1–4)

God has spoken in Christ. This is the final word, the fulfillment
of the law. If the first revelation came with a warning, how much
more should we heed the final revelation in God's Son?

This final revelation, in common with the rest of the New
Testament, is wisdom with a Trinitarian shape. It is a speaking
of the Father in the Son (Heb. 1:1; 2:3) that still speaks today by
the Spirit (2:4; 10:15). This wisdom relates, as we saw in Paul, to
the death of Christ, which in Hebrews cleanses from sin (1:3). It
invites us to participate fully in Christ (3:14) and to imitate the way
of the cross (12:1–2). This wisdom transforms us into the image
of God (2:10–11; 12:7–11). God's wisdom has its primary locus
in the church (12:23), but one day it will bring the entire created
order to bow before the Son. Related to that day, here is the warning: some will bow in worship, others in judgment (12:25–29).
This is the author's warning to the Hebrew Christians. We, too,
should not assume that we have faithfully and fully entered into

13. For the emphasis on educational language in Hebrews 5:11–14, see O'Brien,
Hebrews, 205–10.

the wisdom of God. Should we not "pay much closer attention" to this speaking of the Father in the Son (2:1)?

Jesus taught us in Matthew 11:25 that those who attend his school of wisdom must be as little children to whom the Father reveals the things of the Son. So like curious and teachable children, let us discover anew from Hebrews what it means to know Christ as our prophet, priest, and king. The Westminster Standards are still worth reviewing on this, especially the ever-delightful *Catechism for Young Children: An Introduction to the Shorter Catechism*.[14]

Wisdom in Christ, the Ultimate Revelation

We begin with Christ as our prophet. The celebration of Christ's unique ability to reveal God is one of the most prominent features of the prologue to Hebrews. The word "prophet" is inadequate to contain the Son's revelatory power. As with so many revelatory figures of the Old Testament, Christ both fulfills and surpasses the prophet's function. This is also why we must read the wisdom of Christ carefully against the background of the Wisdom figure. God's revelatory wisdom in his Son far exceeds that of both the Old Testament prophets and Lady Wisdom.

Literary Structure and the Prophetic Function

The compositional centers of New Testament Christological passages are often their theological heart.[15] We saw this in Colossians 1:15–20, with the expression "all things hold together" in the Son (1:17); in Philippians 2:5–11, where Christ's way of

14. See the *Catechism for Young Children: An Introduction to the Shorter Catechism*, http://www.reformed.org/documents/cat_for_young_children.html, questions 64–71; see also Joel R. Beeke and Sinclair B. Ferguson, eds., *Reformed Confessions Harmonized* (Grand Rapids: Baker, 1999), 69–71, for the Westminster Shorter Catechism, questions 23–26, with Scripture, and the Westminster Larger Catechism, questions 43–45, with Scripture.

See questions 64–71; also the Westminster Shorter Catechism, questions 23–26, with Scripture; and the Westminster Larger Catechism, questions 42–45, with Scripture.

15. Cf. Victor Wilson, *Divine Symmetries: The Art of Biblical Rhetoric* (Lanham, MD: University Press of America, 1997), 49.

humble obedience led to death, "even death on a cross" (2:8); and in John 1, where the center contained the invitation's promise: "to all who did receive him, who believed in his name, he gave the right to become children of God" (1:12). In the same way, the author of Hebrews has deliberately shaped his central lines, this time to emphasize the Son as God's supreme self-expression. These statements portray the Son in relation to both the Father and the universe. They are the theological basis for the Son's unique ability to be the perfect revealer of God and Mediator of the new covenant.

> He is the radiance of the glory of God
>> and the exact imprint of his nature,
> and he upholds the universe
>> by the word of his power. (Heb. 1:3a–b)

The Son's Revelatory Power in Relation to the Identity of God

In his first proposition, the author describes the Son as "the radiance of the glory of God." The word "radiance" translates a word that suggests the shining out of light. This is what led to the expression "light out of light" being etched into the Nicene Creed.[16] The second proposition declares that the Son is "the exact imprint of his [God's] nature." In both of these expressions the author, although using his own distinctive vocabulary, is building on the received Christian tradition concerning God's Son.

God's self-revelation in the Old Testament was appropriately described as the manifestation of wisdom, and this was sometimes represented as Wisdom personified (Prov. 1, 9). The type of language used in the intertestamental period to describe this figure in relation to God, especially in the Wisdom of Solomon, is similar to the language used to describe the Son in relation to the Father. The language is not exactly the same, and the function of Lady Wisdom in Pseudo-Solomon falls far short of the

---

16. "I believe . . . in one Lord Jesus Christ, the only-begotten Son of God, begotten of the Father before all worlds; God of God, Light of Light, very God of very God; begotten, not made, being of one substance with the Father, by whom all things were made."

function of the Son in Hebrews. It is theologically sound to think of God's speaking in his Son as the culmination both of the Old Testament speaking and of wisdom itself. However, the influence of the Wisdom figure on New Testament Christology, especially as wisdom speculation developed during the Second Temple period, should not be exaggerated.[17]

The early church confessed that Christ was the "image" of the invisible God (Col. 1:15). Such Christological themes presupposed the Son's divine identity, but they were not merely ontological. They also spoke of the Son in his unique revelatory capacity. Paul captures this connection when he describes his message as "the light of the gospel of the glory of Christ, who is the image of God" (2 Cor. 4:4). This applies directly to us: "For God, who said, 'Let light shine out of darkness,' has shone in our hearts to give the light of the knowledge of the glory of God in the face of Jesus Christ" (2 Cor. 4:6). The author of Hebrews presents his theology on this same conceptual terrain. While these propositions are a confession of the deity of the Son, we must not miss their revelatory emphasis. This is how the Son is our wisdom: he gives us insight, understanding, and knowledge of the living God and his ways.

The Son's Revelatory Power in Relation to the Universe

The first two lines of the prologue's literary center describe the Son's revelatory power in relation to God. The second two lines add a third proposition: the Son "upholds the universe by the word of his power." Recognizing that the author has set this second set of lines in deliberate tandem with the first (see the layout above) is important for several reasons. Their parallel features are what give cohesion to this central core of the composition.[18]

17. The lines in Hebrews 1:3 should not be read as influenced directly by Jewish wisdom speculation. But see Lane, *Hebrews 1–8*, 3–19 and cxxxix. The author is building directly on early-church Christology, which had already developed well beyond Jewish wisdom speculation. For a sustained argument on this with regard to Hebrews, see Ebert, "Wisdom in New Testament Christology," especially chapter 3. The argument is summarized in O'Brien, *Hebrews*, 53–54.

18. The parallelism is best seen in the original language. Four features should be noted. (1) There is euphony in the Greek between the opening sounds of each set of

It is around this central nucleus that the rest of the confession falls into near-perfect symmetry.

Furthermore, the author's tight alignment of these lines draws attention to an often-overlooked but fundamental point: the Son as a person can be distinguished from the powerful divine word ("the word of his power"), which he exerts in sustaining the universe. The Son is distinguished from God the Father, being the radiance and exact imprint of his reality, yet at the same time exercises God's word of providential power. The Jewish Wisdom figure, which is sometimes personified as God's creative word and power, is never a distinct person who exercises that same divine word.

In this sense, the New Testament has moved far beyond wisdom speculation. The Son, as we saw in Colossians 1:17 and as we find here in Hebrews 1:3, is the sustaining and guiding center of the universe. He encompasses all that was ever said of Wisdom in relation to the created order because he is the divine Son of God. We have here the doctrinal tissue of Trinitarian theology.

The Son's Revelatory Power in Relation to Prophets and Angels

Is the author's emphasis here on the Son's nature as God or on his revelatory function and capacity? The former is a clear entailment of how the early church understood God's identity as Father, Son, and Spirit.[19] However, the entire shape of the prologue, including this internal core, draws our attention to the Son's revelatory role.

This is confirmed when we look at the beginning and end of the composition:

> Long ago, at many times and in many ways, God spoke to our fathers by the prophets, but in these last days he has spoken to

---

lines, and between the closing sounds of each set. (2) The verbs found here are the only present tenses in the prologue. (3) The first couplet contains ten words in the Greek and the second, nine words. (4) The lines focus on revelatory phenomena in relation to God: radiance, exact imprint, and word.

19. Evidence that the author of Hebrews presupposed Christ's deity includes references to Christ as God (1:5–10 and possibly 3:3–4); references to the incarnation (1:6; 2:9, 14–16; 10:5–7); and references to Christ's eternal nature (1:10–12; 7:3; 13:8).

us by his Son, . . . having become as much superior to angels as
the name he has inherited is more excellent than theirs.

Our powers of concentration are tested by a sentence as
complex and rich as Hebrews 1:1–4. In the midst of the detail, we
must not miss the author's main point. It is the announcement
of revelation par excellence: God has spoken by his Son! This is
the quintessential revelation—a revelation for the "last days," a
revelation "to us," a revelation that fulfills and supersedes the Old
Testament prophetic word. Here is both canonical continuity and
glorious discontinuity.

There is continuity because it is God who has spoken on
both occasions; he spoke to our spiritual ancestors, and he spoke
through those who were truly prophets. The apostle Paul writes
in Romans that God promised the gospel "beforehand through
his prophets in the holy Scriptures" (Rom. 1:2), and that "the
Law and the Prophets bear witness" to the gospel (3:21). There is
discontinuity, because now God has spoken in one who is his Son.
John put it this way in his prologue: "the law was given through
Moses; grace and truth came through Jesus Christ. No one has
ever seen God; the only God, who is at the Father's side, he has
made him known" (John 1:17–18).

When the author of Hebrews rounds out his prologue in
verse 4, he returns to Christ's supreme revelatory capacity; only
now, the Son is contrasted with the angels. The sudden reference
to angels can be confusing for the modern reader. Several points
help us understand why the author concludes his prologue this
way: (1) angels are by definition messengers; (2) angels played
a special role in the revelation of the old covenant (Heb. 2:2; cf.
Acts 7:38–39; Gal. 3:19);[20] and (3) Christ is going to be presented
in the rest of Hebrews as the Mediator of a new covenant. The
argument, embedded symmetrically at the beginning, center, and
conclusion of the prologue, is powerful: prophets (Heb. 1:1) and
angels (1:4) mediated the old covenant; but Jesus, because of
his nature and revelatory capacity as God's own Son, is superior

20. See O'Brien, *Hebrews*, 62 and n116, for references in extrabiblical Jewish literature.

(1:3a–b). This is the revelatory foundation for Jesus' mediation of the new covenant. Jesus is God's own Son, and God has now spoken through him.

How Is Christ a Prophet?

Is it any wonder that the word "prophet" cannot contain the Son's revelatory power? Christ simply cannot be adequately explained by prior categories of revelation (the Jewish Wisdom figure, angels, or prophets). But if we understand "prophet" as a metaphor for revelation, we can return to the question of the child's catechism, "How is Christ a prophet?" We could legitimately ask the question this way: "How is Christ our wisdom?"

The child's response to this question is simple and yet profound: "Because he teaches us the will of God." New Testament Christology argues that Jesus is qualified to do this because he is the eternal Son of God, imaging God's own being and sustaining the universe by his word. He is better than the messengers of old, including prophets and angels. He teaches us God's will because in these last days God has spoken to us through him.

The Father provides this revelation graciously to those who come to Christ as children, trusting, humble, and teachable. Children are asked, "Why do you need Christ as a prophet?" We should not cringe at the catechism's answer: "Because I am ignorant!" Is the church still teachable in the school of Christ's wisdom? Christology was confessed as wisdom to meet the needs of New Testament churches. Careful reflection on God's revelation in Christ can still meet our needs today.

The theme of the prophetic office of Christ should also help us to understand the mission of the church in the world.[21] Our calling includes the prophetic activity of teaching God's will revealed through Christ, both by our words and by our collective lives transformed by the gospel. As he is the light

---

21. For the suggestion that the three offices of Christ have implications for the mission of the church, see Daniel L. Migliore, *Faith Seeking Understanding: An Introduction to Christian Theology*, 2nd ed. (Grand Rapids: Eerdmans, 2004), 266 and n30.

of the world (John 1:9), so we are to shine "as lights in the world, holding fast to the word of life" (Phil. 2:15–16). This can also be expressed in terms of wisdom. Christ through his incarnation was the supreme embodiment of divine wisdom, and calls us to learn from him (Matt. 11:29). The content of this wisdom centers on the gospel and the crucifixion of Christ (1 Cor. 1), as well as the new way of life that Christ modeled for us (Phil. 2). At his ascension, the Lord sent his Spirit, the Spirit of wisdom, to dwell within us, and to proclaim this message to the world (1 Cor. 2).

Wisdom in Christ, the Efficacious Redeemer

Christ's priestly work is the main doctrinal theme of Hebrews. In the body of his epistle, the author will teach several important truths concerning Christ's priesthood, the most important of which include the following:

1. Jesus' priestly work is effective because he accomplishes it as the Son of God with eternal power (7:3, 16).
2. Christ has been explicitly appointed by God to do the work of a priest, which is to offer sacrifice for sin (5:1), as a priest after the order of Melchizedek (7:1–28).
3. His priestly work is perfect, and as a result he has taken his seat at God's right hand (10:12–14; 8:1).

Remarkably, the author has quietly planted all the seeds for this presentation of Jesus as priest within the prologue.

Literary Structure and the Priesthood

The line that refers to purification (1:3) is the only explicit reference to Jesus' priestly work in Hebrews 1:1–4. But the literary structure, the flow of the syntax, and the biblical allusions all combine to lay the groundwork, subtly but effectively, for the author's teaching on Christ's priesthood. The clause concerning

157

the cleansing of sin and its parallel clause are graphically displayed below (highlighted in italics):

> whom he appointed the heir of all things [Ps. 2:8],
>> *through whom also he created* [literally *"made"*] *the world*.
>>> He is the radiance of the glory of God
>>>> and the exact imprint of his nature,
>>> and he upholds the universe
>>>> by the word of his power.
>> *After making purification for sins*,
> he sat down at the right hand of the Majesty on high [Ps. 110:1].

The Son of God as Powerful Priest

While the primary structural focus of the prologue is on the messianic Son's revelatory power, his priestly work is intentionally woven into the structure. The author does this in a way that brings Jesus' redemptive work into striking juxtaposition with his divine identity as the Son of God, including his cosmic work as Creator and as sovereign sustainer of the universe. The subject of this line is the Son in whom God has spoken, and who has been identified as sharing in the divine identity (Heb. 1:3a–b). The parallel line earlier in the chiastic structure reminds the reader that the one who *made* cleansing for sin is the same powerful one through whom God *made* the world. Not only this, but the preceding clause shows this same agent of creation to be the one who by the word of divine power providentially "upholds the universe." It is this one, the Son of God, who accomplished the priestly task of offering a sacrifice for the purification of sins (5:1–10). This identification of the eschatological Great High Priest as the Son of God is critical to the author's argument.[22]

The Messianic Son as Appointed Priest

One of the unique contributions of Hebrews to New Testament Christology is its identification of Jesus, the Son of God, as

22. See Heb. 4:14; 5:5, 8; 7:3, 28.

a priest after the order of Melchizedek (Heb. 7; cf. 5:6, 10; 6:20). This is effectively, although indirectly, embedded in the prologue. The author alludes to two messianic psalms in the prologue. These are found in the parallel lines indicated in italics below:

> *whom he appointed the heir of all things* [Ps. 2:8],
>> through whom also he created [literally "made"] the world.
>>> He is the radiance of the glory of God
>>>> and the exact imprint of his nature,
>>> and he upholds the universe
>>>> by the word of his power.
>> After making purification for sins,
> *he sat down at the right hand of the Majesty on high* [Ps. 110:1].

Both of these psalms were recognized in the early church as messianic and fulfilled by Jesus.[23] The author of Hebrews creatively brings them into alignment in his prologue to celebrate the Son's messianic role.[24] But he has another purpose as well. He intends to bring these two psalms together again in chapter 5. Only this time, by shifting to verse 7 in Psalm 2 and by shifting to verse 4 in Psalm 110, he will prove that Jesus, as the Son of God, is also appointed a priest forever after the order of Melchizedek (Heb. 5:4–6).

> And no one takes this honor for himself, but only when called
>> by God . . . So also
> Christ did not exalt himself to be made a high priest, but was
>> appointed by him who said to him,

> "You are my Son,
> today I have begotten you" [Ps. 2:7];
> as he says also in another place,

> "You are a priest forever,
> after the order of Melchizedek" [Ps. 110:4].

23. Psalm 2 is applied to Jesus in the believers' prayer in Acts 4:26.
24. The author brings these two psalms into alignment again in his treatment of the Son and angels in Hebrews 1:5–13 by beginning (Ps. 2:7) and ending (Ps. 110:1) the list of Old Testament citations with their explicit quotation.

By introducing these same psalms in the prologue, the author anticipates this important teaching on Christ's priesthood, which he will develop throughout his epistle.

The Exalted Son as Efficacious Priest

The author's purpose for introducing his teaching concerning Christ's priesthood is also confirmed by the syntactical order in the prologue: "after making purification for sins, [the Son] sat down at the right hand of the Majesty on high" (1:3c–d). For the author, these two steps belong together and are wrapped up with Jesus' priestly work. Under the new covenant (8:6–13), and with reference to the heavenly tabernacle (9:1–12), Jesus first suffered for sins and then sat down at God's right hand (10:12). Here, within the inner place of the sanctuary, Jesus is our Great High Priest after the order of Melchizedek (6:19–20; cf. 4:14–16). The result of the Son's priestly work is that he has obtained our "eternal redemption" (9:12) by his own blood—"the blood of the eternal covenant" (13:20).

Here is Christology at its best, creatively and effectively applied to meet the needs of the early church. Although they had lost the benefits of the earthly temple, with its priesthood and sacrifices, they had gained the better benefits of the perfect heavenly ministry of Christ. The apostle calls on them, and on us, to "consider Jesus, the apostle and high priest of our confession" (Heb. 3:1). This is what it means to continue in Christ's school of wisdom in the midst of extreme difficulty. If wisdom is found in Christ and the gospel, then every difficulty of life should drive the church to reflect more deeply on the meaning of God's revelation in his Son.

How Is Christ a Priest?

The child responds to this question of the catechism: "Because he died for our sins and pleads with God for us." Hebrews will unveil that this death for sins was an efficacious priestly sacrifice, and that Christ is now seated at God's own right hand as our sympathetic Great High Priest. All this has been hinted at in Hebrews 1:1–4.

The child is pressed, "Why do I need Christ as a priest?" The answer is straightforward: "Because I am sinful." Repentance and faith are still signs of the presence of the kingdom of Christ, and the way of entrance to the rest that is salvation. The call of wisdom is still a call, not to those who are strong and proud but to those who are broken and teachable. The warning of Hebrews 2:1 should echo in our ears: "Let us pay much closer attention!"

Again, the theme of the priestly office of Christ should help us to understand the mission of the church in the world. As his disciples, we are to function as a kingdom of priests, offering sacrifices of praise that confess his name (Heb. 13:15; 1 Peter 2:5), making sacrifices of goodness and sharing with others (Heb. 13:16), and doing the priestly work of announcing forgiveness and reconciliation in Christ (Heb. 13:16; 1 Peter 2:9). This mission of compassion and reconciliation is the way of life for those shaped by the wisdom of Christ. We saw this exemplified in our study of 1 Corinthians, Colossians, and Philippians.

Wisdom in Christ, the Supreme Ruler

Jesus is our prophet and priest, and also our king. We considered how the author's allusions to Psalm 2 and Psalm 110 prepared for his identification of God's Son as a priest after the order of Melchizedek. We now look at these two psalms in their primary focus on Christ's rule.

Literary Structure and the Royal-Priestly Rule

Because of the parallelism and the relationship of these two lines to the flow of the syntax, the relevant lines are again displayed in italics:

whom he appointed the heir of all things [Ps. 2:8],
    through whom also he created [literally "made"] the world.

He is the radiance of the glory of God
and the exact imprint of his nature,
and he upholds the universe
by the word of his power.
After making purification for sins,
he sat down at the right hand of the Majesty on high [Ps. 110:1].

The Function of Psalm 2

This is one of the key Old Testament texts taken up by Jesus and the earliest church, and serves as part of the New Testament's Christological substructure.[25] The author of Hebrews uses this psalm in a unique way—to link the Son of God as royal Messiah with the Son of God as High Priest. The allusion to Psalm 2 sets the stage for this important Christological move.

The psalmist explicitly declares that the Messiah (the Lord's anointed [2:2]) is God's Son (2:7, 12).[26] This is central to Jesus' identity. The public declaration that Christ the Messiah is the Father's own Son is associated in the life of Jesus with his baptism (Matt. 3:17), his transfiguration (Matt. 17:5; 2 Peter 1:13), and his resurrection (Rom. 1:3–4). A fundamental premise of the church's Christological confession, therefore, was that Jesus is both God's Son and the anointed king.[27] His kingdom has been inaugurated, although earthly powers still rage against him (Acts 4:25–27). His kingdom is about to be consummated, as the seventh angel in the book of Revelation announces: "The kingdom of the world has become the kingdom of our Lord and of his Christ [alluding to Ps. 2:2], and he will reign for ever and ever" (Rev. 11:15). The author of Hebrews and the early church held this in common. It is to this royal Son that the Father says, "Ask of me, and I will make the nations your heritage, and the ends of the earth your possession" (Ps. 2:8). The author brings Psalm 2 into play

25. See the still-important study of C. H. Dodd, *According to the Scriptures: The Substructure of New Testament Theology* (London: Nisbet, 1953).

26. Other psalms identify the Davidic king as God's "anointed" (Ps. 18:50; 20:6; 45:7; especially 89:20), but it is Psalm 2 that uniquely identifies the Son of God as the anointed king.

27. Note the confession of Nathanael: "Rabbi, you are the Son of God! You are the King of Israel!" (John 1:49).

by echoing it with his line: "whom he appointed the heir of all things" (Heb. 1:2b).

The Time of the Royal Inheritance

There are two further questions that we need to address with regard to his first citation. When did this inheritance take place? And why is it followed by a reference to the Son's creative work?

The time of the Son's inheritance, mentioned in Hebrews 1:2b, has been contested. The older view was that this referred to the eternal declaration of God. The current majority position is that this declaration coincides with the Son's exaltation (i.e., it occurred at the same time as the heavenly session in Hebrews 1:3d). There are elements in the text that point to the Son's pre-temporal existence. The creative fiat itself hints at the Son's preexistence. The "world" that he creates is literally "the ages," which is suggestive of "time-space reality." Furthermore, his relationship to the Father at the center of the composition also leads to the possibility of a reference to an inheritance decree rooted in eternity.

However, there are other textual indicators that point to a temporal inheritance. The Davidic psalm itself is prophetic of Christ's life and ministry. The early church understood this psalm as fulfilled in the events of Jesus' life. The prologue of Hebrews begins with the announcement of God's speaking in the Son "in these last days," which suggests an eschatological orientation. Finally, the parallel event in verse 3 with its royal-priestly ascension seems to favor the exaltation as the time of the inheritance. As it is so often with these kinds of issues, the question may be misleading. For example, does the Son as image or form of God in Colossians and Philippians refer to the Son's ontological identity with God or to his revelatory function in human history? The answer is best seen as both: his ontological identity with God is what ultimately grounds his revelatory function. The Son's divine right as heir of all creation, in fellowship with the Father and the Spirit, is the basis of his function as the incarnate and exalted king,

163

who becomes the messianic heir of all. The author's emphasis is on the exaltation, but when we probe it deep enough, it leads to Trinitarian implications.

But why, in the order of the text, does the author refer to the creation *after* the reference to inheritance? Notice the order of the two lines here (Heb. 1:2b–c):

> whom he appointed the heir of all things [Ps. 2:8],
> through whom also he made the world.

The second line can seem like an afterthought. If the focus is on his inheritance at the exaltation, why go back in the next line and mention that he is the Creator? The author does this for two reasons. First, Christ's position as heir is related to his creative work. This, too, is part of the early church's confessional material: everything was created through him (John 1:3; 1 Cor. 8:6) and *for* him (Col. 1:16). But why present these in the inverted order? Why not say that he created the world, and therefore inherits it? The answer lies in the literary structure and rhetorical purpose of the author. The lines are ordered this way because of the composition's concentric structure: the author wants to set in tandem the two lines that echo the psalms (2 and 110) and the two lines that refer to what the Son has "made" (the worlds, and cleansing for sin). Furthermore, and more importantly, the author wants to make the following argument: as the Son's creative work led eventually to his kingly reign as heir, so his redemptive work led to his priestly reign at the Father's right hand.

The Function of Psalm 110

This messianic psalm, even more than Psalm 2, is a critical element in the Old Testament substructure to the gospel message.[28] Its use can be traced to Jesus, who asked the Pharisees how the Messiah could be David's son, since David called him "Lord" in

28. For important bibliography on Psalm 110's use in the New Testament, see O'Brien, *Hebrews*, 59n99.

Psalm 110:1. The implication was that Christ was the Son of God and not merely David's son (Matt. 22:41–46). In Peter's sermon at Pentecost we read:

> This Jesus God raised up, and of that we all are witnesses. Being therefore exalted at the right hand of God, and having received from the Father the promise of the Holy Spirit, he has poured out this that you yourselves are seeing and hearing. For David did not ascend into the heavens, but he himself says,
>
> "The Lord said to my Lord,
> 'Sit at my right hand,
> until I make your enemies your footstool.'"
>
> Let all the house of Israel therefore know for certain that God has made him both Lord and Christ, this Jesus whom you crucified. (Acts 2:32–36)

While Psalm 2 is a highly significant Old Testament text in Hebrews, Psalm 110 is *the* most important text for the author. The roots of his priestly Christology most likely lie in early Christian reflection on this psalm. Peter O'Brien nicely summarizes an important study on this phenomenon by D. M. Hays:

> Some thirty-three quotations or allusions to Ps. 110 (vv. 1 and 4) are scattered throughout the New Testament, occurring in a range of contexts that point to Jesus or Christians being seated at the right hand of God (Rom. 8:34; Eph. 1:20; Col. 3:1; Mark 14:62, etc.), where affirmations are made about the subjection of the powers to Christ (1 Cor. 15:25; Eph. 1:20; Heb. 10:12–13; Rev. 3:21), and where statements are made in connection with Jesus' intercession and priestly office (Rom. 8:34; Heb. 7:25).[29]

For the author of Hebrews, Psalm 110 becomes the theological linchpin of his epistle and the source of his unique Christological contribution. The author will cite Psalm 110:1 later, in

29. O'Brien, *Hebrews*, 59n101.

Hebrews 1:13, and will allude to it in chapters 8, 10, and 12. More significant is the author's move to verse 4 of the psalm for his exposition of Jesus' high priestly ministry. In fact, one could argue that the author never alludes to Psalm 110:1 without associating it with the implications of Psalm 110:4 (see 8:1; 10:12; 12:2). This is why he introduces it here in the prologue.

To unpack what the author is doing with the allusion to Psalm 110:1, we need to consider: (1) the flow of the sentence grammatically; (2) two important theological assumptions; and (3) the impact of the literary structure.

With the shift of subjects at the center from the Father to the Son (Heb. 1:3), the sentence structure tilts forward to the main verb, which is found in the clause under consideration. Remember, there is only one sentence in the Greek. In a sense, the entire prologue could be reduced to the core sentence: God has spoken by his Son (main verb in vv. 1–2), who sat down (main verb in vv. 3–4). Everything else amplifies this basic statement. The following layout, with slight modifications of the ESV translation, helps to bring out this feature. Note the core sentence in italics.

> Long ago, at many times and in many ways,
> *God* having spoken to our fathers by the prophets,
> . . . in these last days *has spoken* to us *by his Son*,
>   whom he appointed the heir of all things (Ps. 2:8),
>   through whom also he created the world,
>   *Who* being the radiance of the glory of God
>   and the exact imprint of his nature,
>   and upholding the universe
>   by the word of his power,
>   After making purification for sins,
> *sat down* at the right hand of the Majesty on high (Ps. 110:1),
>   having become as much superior to angels
> as the name he has inherited is more excellent than theirs.

Looking at the core sentence this way helps us to see the importance of Psalm 110:1. The early church would immediately affirm this as the exaltation of the royal Son.

There are two narrative assumptions here that the early church would have also immediately supplied, although more liberal scholars have sometimes made too much of their absence from the prologue: the incarnation and the resurrection. This is why it is so important to read these New Testament passages in light of the early church's shared Christological confession. To read the prologue as though somehow these ideas were absent or unimportant to the author is to misread his theological context and the basic gospel narrative. The incarnation will, in fact, be explicit in the argument of Hebrews 2, and the resurrection will be celebrated in the great benediction of Hebrews 13:20–21.

Hebrews confesses with the rest of the New Testament that Jesus is the incarnate Son of God who died on the cross to atone for sin. These confessional elements distinguish the author's Christology from Jewish wisdom speculation. The Wisdom figure is never said to have taken on flesh and blood (2:14), nor to have died on a cross to atone for sin (9:12; 12:2).[30]

For rhetorical reasons, the author's focus in the prologue is neither on the incarnation nor on the cross itself. His emphasis is on Jesus' purification for sins and exaltation to God's right hand. Hebrews is subtly introducing the Son's exaltation in terms of his priestly ministry. This is effectively done by the preceding line, which declared that the Son had made purification for sin, *and* by the allusion to Psalm 110:1. This psalm contains the motif of Christ's priesthood after the order of Melchizedek (Ps. 110:4), later to be developed by the author. It also contains the invitation for the Messiah, having accomplished his work, to sit down (Ps. 110:1). The Son is messianic king, as confessed by the early church, but he is an enthroned royal priest as well.

From the perspective of the epistle's doctrinal emphasis, these two clauses ("after making purification for sins" and "sat down"), taken together, are the climax of the prologue. The purging of sins by the incarnate Son's sacrifice and his present priestly ministry in heaven are at the heartbeat of God's final self-disclosure.

30. Ebert, "Wisdom," 110; and see O'Brien, *Hebrews*, 54 and n67.

There is another component of the author's prologue that is important. This messianic figure, who is both king and priest, is none other than the powerful Son of God. He is the agent of creation, and so the rightful heir; he is the one who upholds the universe by the divine word. This is the same one who is the powerful agent of redemption, and who resides at the place of power, even God's own right hand. Here we return to the motif of the Son as the ultimate ruler.

The author of Hebrews has squarely set his introduction to Christ within the context of the early Christian confession that Jesus is exalted and reigning at God's right hand. While his focus is on the priestly work of Christ, it is the work of the Son who is the sovereign king. He is a king of righteousness and peace (cf. Heb. 7:1–2). He is a king who is identified with God himself. In the section immediately following the prologue, where Christ is extensively contrasted with angels, we read: "But of the Son he says, 'Your throne, O God, is forever and ever, the scepter of uprightness is the scepter of your kingdom'" (1:8).

Once the author has fully established that the messianic and royal Son is also priest, his Christology shifts away from a focus on the title "Son of God" to a focus on his priesthood.[31] However, the title "Son" is used again, in Hebrews 7:3 and 7:28, where the Son's eternal priesthood is at issue.[32] The full messianic title "Son of God" is also used in Hebrews 6:6 and Hebrews 10:29, where warning is given against rejecting Jesus' sacrificial work.

The warning to respond properly to the kingly rule of Christ is a call to wisdom. Psalm 2 puts it this way:

Now therefore, O kings, *be wise*; be warned, O rulers of the earth. Serve the Lord with fear, and rejoice with trembling. Kiss the Son, lest he be angry, and you perish in the way, for his wrath is quickly kindled. Blessed are all who take refuge in him. (Ps. 2:10–12)

31. This occurs after Hebrews 5:8.
32. There is also an indirect emphasis in chapter 7 on the Son's kingly role, since Melchizedek's name contains the word "king," and he was king of Salem.

The author of Hebrews likewise encourages us:

> Therefore let us be grateful for receiving a kingdom that cannot
> be shaken, and thus let us offer to God acceptable worship,
> with reverence and awe, for our God is a consuming fire.
> (Heb. 12:28–29)

How Is Christ a King?

In the catechism's treatment of Christ's three offices, the final
set of questions relates to kingship. Children confess that Christ is
king "because he rules over us and defends us." In response to the
question why he or she needs Christ as king, each child confesses,
"Because I am weak and helpless." Hebrews reveals to us that
this king is none other than the powerful Son of God, even God
himself. He is powerful, both creating the world and sustaining
it. He will one day shake the heavens and earth in judgment. But
wrapped up with his power is his compassion, revealed in his
incarnation and sympathetic priestly ministry. Blessed, indeed,
are all who take refuge in him (Ps. 2:12)!

The motif of the Son's kingship, as with his prophetic and
priestly offices, spills over into the church. Our reign is one that
is caught between the times of the exaltation of Christ at his
ascension, and his return to establish his eternal kingdom. We
live "in these last days" (Heb. 1:1), waiting "till his enemies be
made his footstool" (1:13; 10:13; cf. 2:8), but we also "have tasted
the powers of the age to come" (6:5), and receive "a kingdom that
cannot be shaken" (12:28). We reign with him provisionally as a
"royal priesthood" (1 Peter 2:9). But one day, persevering in faith,
we will fully reign with Christ in his consummated kingdom.
We will rule with authority, even as the Son was given authority
(Rev. 2:26–27, citing Ps. 2).

Whenever we think of Christological rule or power, it must
be informed by the counterintuitive nature of God's wisdom and
power in Christ. Today our kingly work imitates Christ's, which
is characterized by peace and righteousness. We reflect the Son's
rule when we live our lives and use our resources to reflect his

inaugurated kingdom—and not least, when we protect and advocate for the "weak and helpless."

Summary of Wisdom in Hebrews

In presenting Christ to us, the author gathers up common confessional elements found in the early church and weaves them together to give us an application of the wisdom of God in Christ. As we have seen in our other texts, this is a Christology that is to be distinguished from intertestamental wisdom speculation. It was designed to meet the needs of a struggling Christian community. The author celebrates the person and work of Christ in a way that might be called a lesson in "advanced wisdom."

Beyond the Wisdom Figure

While the prologue to Hebrews contains an amazing celebration of Christological wisdom, it builds on elements that are foreign to the Jewish Wisdom figure (e.g., the incarnation and resurrection).[33] The prologue also teaches lessons that go beyond what could ever be said of Lady Wisdom. Here are three examples that we saw:

1. Hebrews deliberately aligns the Son's roles as Creator and Redeemer.
2. Hebrews portrays a nuanced relationship between the Son and the Father.
3. Hebrews distinguishes subtly between the Son and the divine word.

If there was a Wisdom strand to the church's earliest Christology, it was so well integrated into the church's confession as to have lost any independent significance. The author's wisdom points in another direction.

33. Ebert, "Wisdom," 110.

Advanced Wisdom

Hebrews builds on traditional early-church Christology to communicate more advanced wisdom concerning Christ's person and work (Heb. 5:11–14). In common with earlier confessional material, Hebrews has masterfully announced God's Son as the supreme revealer of God, the powerfully qualified Redeemer, and the exalted messianic king. Jesus *is* our prophet, priest, and king!

The author's unique insight, however, is the identification of the divine Son explicitly and directly as High Priest, which he will develop throughout his epistle. He applies his Christology this way to help the community persevere in their faith.

To know Christ in all his wisdom as our prophet, priest, and king means that we not only enter into the blessings of Christ, but reflect this wisdom in the way we live in the world. We are to share Christ with all who will listen to wisdom's call; we are to proclaim the good news of the forgiveness of sins, all the while modeling lives of reconciliation; and we are to exercise power and authority as joint heirs with Christ in ways that are merciful and just.

Melanchthon, an important church Reformer, wrote, "To know Christ is to know his benefits."[34] The author of Hebrews is confident that if we truly come to know Christ, we will persevere in our faith and fully participate in his benefits. This is the purpose of his "word of exhortation" (13:22). In the language of the rest of his epistle, God's wisdom in his Son, our Great High Priest, calls us to hold fast to the faith (4:14); to draw near to God in worship (10:22); and to go on to maturity (6:1). This is the apostolic pattern of calling the church to faithfully confess Christ, who is God's wisdom for us.

---

34. The quote comes from Philipp Melanchthon's *Loci communes*, often regarded as the first Protestant systematic theology.

Conclusion: Learning to Live in the Wisdom of Christ

TODAY, KNOWLEDGE has far outpaced wisdom. The problems this creates are apparent all around us. We have ATM cards and online banking, but our society struggles with an unprecedented debt problem that has become a form of bondage. Quantum leaps forward in our knowledge of disease, along with new medical technologies, have increased life expectancy, but where is the wisdom for heart-rending decisions about the end of life? The Internet and globalization have brought diverse cultures into a new era of human civilization. But without wisdom, the fabric of society threatens to unravel, leaving unanswered fundamental questions about what it means to be family, neighbors, and human beings who can discern between good and evil. Our world is hungry for wisdom.

Many are beginning to recognize that biblical wisdom can be a rich resource for contemporary life. It has become a popular motif recently for theology in general, for feminist studies, for mysticism, and for the study of world religions.[1] Because it is such a needed virtue, and because a metaphor such as "Lady Wisdom" is so powerful, it is critical that biblical wisdom be interpreted faithfully.[2]

1. For theology in general, see David Ford, *Christian Wisdom: Desiring God and Learning in Love* (Cambridge: Cambridge University Press, 2007). The interest in Lady Wisdom for feminist theologians continues to grow; for a broadly evangelical example, see Lilian Barger, *Chasing Sophia: Reclaiming the Lost Wisdom of Jesus* (San Francisco: Joseey-Bass, 2007). For mysticism and world religions, see the writings of the Trappist monk Thomas Merton. A recent biography is Christopher Pramuk, *Sophia: The Hidden Christ of Thomas Merton* (Collegeville, MN: Liturgical Press, 2009).

2. A note of caution comes from the historical observation that the heretical movement known as Gnosticism showed the greatest interest in "Sophia" or Lady Wisdom

In the preceding chapters we explored God's wisdom in Christ by a close reading of selected New Testament passages. In conclusion we will summarize our findings and their relevance for the church and her mission in the world.

We begin with a summary of wisdom in the New Testament, describing Christological wisdom in narrative form and then offering a brief theological synthesis. Next we turn to our selected New Testament passages and review how this unique wisdom functioned in each historical situation. Finally, we list some of the more important practical lessons derived from our study, and conclude with a summons to Christ's school of wisdom.

- What Is Wisdom in Christ?
- How Does Wisdom in Christ Work?
- What Does Wisdom in Christ Teach Us?
- Why Seek Wisdom in Christ?

What Is Wisdom in Christ?

Wisdom in the New Testament is both simple and profound. To state it simply: God's wisdom is Christ and the gospel (1 Cor. 1:24, 30). But such a simple confession leads to more wonderful truths and an indescribable wisdom. If such a Christology were stated in all its richness, "even the whole world would not have room for the books that would be written" (John 21:25). The contours of this wisdom are shaped by the gospel and encompass Christ's role in revelation, creation, and redemption.

Narrative Summary of God's Wisdom in Christ

We have discovered that wisdom involves the eternal Son of God, his intimate relationship with the Father, and the triune

---

in the post-New Testament period, and the Sophia language shifted to Mariology in the Middle Ages.

174

life that they share with the Spirit. It involves the Son's work of creation and his exercise of divine power in the preservation and providential direction of the universe. It is the fulfillment of God's promises to Israel, inaugurating the messianic kingdom. It is manifest in Christ's incarnation as an expression of God's love for the world, which leads to the life of Jesus as God's perfect image in human form. Its narrative center is our Lord's death on the cross and, through this, the reconciliation of heaven and earth. It involves the sending of the Spirit, after the Lord's resurrection and ascension, to apply Christ's saving work in the lives of believers, and to create a community of people who reflect God's will and way for the whole world. It culminates in the ascension and glorification of the Son, as well as in the promise of a final cosmic renewal. Wisdom involves all of this and more.

Theological Summary of Christ's Role as Wisdom

The relation of Christ to the phenomenon of wisdom is complex, especially as wisdom is expressed in both the Old Testament and Second Temple Judaism. There is a sense in which Jesus' teaching ministry reflected that of a sage or wisdom teacher, but it was much more. There is a sense in which the form (e.g., parables, sayings) and content (e.g., the invitation to wisdom, the two paths) of his teaching paralleled that of antecedent Jewish wisdom. His teaching was also like that of a prophet, and in other ways it was unique (e.g., his claim to sonship, and the cry of "Abba! Father!").

The relationship of Christ to the personification of Wisdom is likewise complex. No attribute of God was expressed in figurative form so powerfully, and developed so thoroughly, as wisdom. One helpful way to summarize Christ's role as wisdom—that captures and yet distinguishes his relation to Lady Wisdom—is around the three themes of revelation, creation, and redemption.

Wisdom and Revelation. In the literature of Israel, the attribute of God's wisdom was personified. She appears in the Old Testament as Lady Wisdom, and is more fully developed in the

175

apocryphal literature. Wisdom is represented as coming from heaven. She reveals God's will and ways, both as that embedded in the created order (general revelation [Job 38; Prov. 8]) and also through the law and Israel's unique history (special revelation [Deut. 4:6; cf. Sir. 24:22]).[3] In Pseudo-Solomon, Wisdom is further described as reflecting God's glory (Wisd. 7:24–26). While this latter document is not canonical, it shows that people continued to reflect on God's revelation in terms of the Wisdom figure.

Like the function of other Old Testament revelatory figures and institutions (e.g., prophets, angels, Torah, temple), the revelatory function of Wisdom reaches its culmination and is surpassed in Christ. To use the vocabulary of the Epistle to the Hebrews, the former figures were good, but Jesus is "superior" (Heb. 1:4). Although it is helpful to see Christ in the light of antecedent revelatory figures such as Wisdom, our focus should remain on the uniqueness of Christ. We should not fail to see what distinguishes him from all others.

In the Old Testament, Wisdom is the personification of an attribute of God, and not a personal being. It can be argued that Lady Wisdom, even in the more fully developed apocryphal literature, never bridged this gap between personification and an actual being. What makes Christ's revelatory power unique and supreme is that he is more than an attribute of the divine nature. He is a person within the triune identity of God. Christ's relation to the Father is explicitly revealed in terms of his "sonship." Whatever else this might reveal to us about the relation between the first and second persons of the Godhead, it surely has revelatory significance: the Son is the image of the Father; he reveals him as no other can.

Wisdom and Creation. A gift that biblical revelation gives to the world is its understanding of creation's rational, moral, and aesthetic structure—a structure grounded in the omnipotence of a personal Creator.[4] In this cosmic context people are created

3. Wisdom is not actually personified in Job 38. For a nuanced discussion of creation as a source of wisdom, see Daniel J. Estes, *Hear, My Son: Teaching and Learning in Proverbs 1–9* (Grand Rapids: Eerdmans, 1997), 87–99.

4. See, for example, Yahweh as Creator of the beauty and order of creation in Psalm 104, a wisdom psalm.

as God's image bearers to be recipients of his revelation and to reflect his glory. Even human history, while focused after the fall on the people of Israel, is for the blessing of the entire created order, including all the nations. In the Old Testament, the origin of this creational design is linked with God's wisdom (Prov. 3:19). It is at the moment of creation that personified Wisdom makes her joyful appearance (Prov. 8:22–31).

The strongest conceptual tie between personified Wisdom and Christ may well be the creational role. When we come to the New Testament, it is Christ who is present with God at the moment of creation (John 1:1–2), and it is Christ who is the agent of creation (John 1:3; 1 Cor. 8:6; Col. 1:16; Heb. 1:2). To an extent Lady Wisdom may function at this point as a type of Christ. However, here too we must carefully attend to Christ's uniqueness in relation to the created order.

Not only was Wisdom represented as playing a role at creation, so was God's creative word, the divine Spirit, and, in rabbinic Judaism, even Torah. These phenomena can also be seen as picturing Christ's function as Creator. More importantly, the nature of Christ's companionship with God at creation far exceeds what was ever said of Lady Wisdom. This can be seen in at least four ways. First, the Son is present as a person and not merely as a literary figure or personification. Second, Wisdom is described as "created," while the Son is eternal and uncreated (Prov. 8:22; cf. Sir. 24:9). Third, the New Testament goes on to connect this companionship at creation with divine identity: not only was the Son "with God" (John 1:1a), he *was* God (John 1:1b). This was never said of Lady Wisdom. Fourth, Christ was not only the agent of creation, but the glorified Son and sovereign Lord over the creation (Phil. 2:11; Col. 1:17-18; Heb. 1:4), which has its goal in him (Col. 1:16).

All that God's wisdom is represented as doing in creation Christ more than accomplishes. The cosmic scope of God's work in the world, both with regard to the created order and with regard to all the nations, will be brought to completion in Christ (Rom. 8:19–22; 16:25–27). This leads us naturally to the third theme.

Wisdom and Redemption. Two factors converge here that especially highlight the uniqueness of God's wisdom in Christ. First, redemption had not been a wisdom theme in the Old Testament, nor in Second Temple Judaism. Second, the unveiling of God's wisdom in Christ and the gospel was, in contrast, profoundly redemptive. This point is critical and accounts for the explosive and counterintuitive nature of God's wisdom in Christ.

In the literature of Israel, personified Wisdom is represented as playing a salvific or saving role in providing insight, revelation, and providential guidance, but not in a redemptive sense. A careful reading of Proverbs 1–9, which "functions as an overview of the themes and priorities of Proverbs," illustrates the point.[5] To read Wisdom's role in terms of redemption is a mistake.[6]

Yet as we have seen, the one point at which Christ is explicitly called the wisdom of God in the New Testament is in relation to his redemptive work on the cross (1 Cor. 1:23–24, 30). This is a function of Christ as wisdom that is not applicable to Lady Wisdom, but it is the pivotal center of God's wisdom in Christ. As we have seen in our study of the New Testament's heightened Christological passages, the cross of Christ is always the defining factor. This leads us back to the gospel narrative and the unique way in which this wisdom is applied in the life of the church.

How Does Wisdom in Christ Work?

The Christology of the New Testament, in its most concentrated form, appears in the shape of confessional material. It is "applied Christology." Elements of God's wisdom in Christ surface as the gospel is addressed to the circumstances faced by the first-century church. Therefore, these passages teach us not only

---

5. Estes, *Hear, My Son*, 18.

6. See, for example, Sharon H. Ringe, *Wisdom's Friends: Community and Christology in the Fourth Gospel* (Louisville: Westminster John Knox Press, 1999), 57–59, who states that in the Wisdom traditions, wisdom's defining vocation is "mediating God's redemptive presence among mankind" (59).

Christology, but patterns of Christian wisdom. Here we will summarize what we have learned through these unique texts.

Wisdom's Invitation

This study began with an invitation. Jesus and the apostle John summoned us to find saving wisdom in Christ and the gospel. The episode in Matthew took place during the life of Jesus, before his death and resurrection. The invitation in John was framed from the perspective of the finished work of Christ and served as an introduction to his gospel. The contexts are different, but the invitation is the same: to come to Christ and participate in his revelation of the Father and in the Son's saving work.

Matthew. Christ gives an invitation to all who would listen. It is an invitation to become Jesus' disciple and to enter his unique school of wisdom. What the Son reveals comes from his shared life with the Father. This way of life provides a restful alternative to the heavy "yoke" of the Mosaic law, and in Matthew it also takes up and fulfills the law. Such wisdom is rejected by the so-called wise and understanding, but wisdom's invitation is received by little children, "gentle and lowly in heart" (Matt. 11:29) like the Lord. This invitation in the context of Matthew's narrative leads to the cross, both for Jesus and for those who followed him, as well as to the rest God promised to his people.

John. In John's prologue we turned from Jesus' summons to the Fourth Gospel's profound introduction to Jesus as God's final message. John's prologue serves as an invitation to trust in Jesus Christ as the eternal Word. Once again we are reminded of the intimate relationship between the Father and the Son. It is the Word, both as preexistent Creator and as incarnate Son, who is fully qualified to reveal the Father and bring us into new life. This invitation entails a move forward from Moses to the grace and truth of the gospel. In both Matthew and John, the emphasis is on the Father's gracious initiative. Not all respond to the wisdom of God revealed in his Son—but those who do experience a new birth and become children of God.

179

Wisdom's Application to Church Life

Our study turned next to a series of passages in which Christological wisdom was used to address a range of problems in the early church.

First Corinthians. A major problem for the church at Corinth was a divisive spirit, caused by pride in human wisdom. In this context, Paul explicitly calls Christ "the wisdom of God." Such wisdom has its foundation in the Son's participation, as "the Lord of Glory," in the identity of God (1 Cor. 2:8; 8:6). Such confessional wisdom is also defined by the Son's sacrificial death for others. The content of this wisdom is Christ and the cross-centered gospel. Identifying "Christ crucified" as God's wisdom sets aside all human wisdom and self-confidence and points us toward the way of the cross as our model for life. To illustrate the ethical implications of this wisdom, Paul applied it to the situation of proud believers who were not properly caring for weaker brothers in the practical matter of meat offered to idols. Believers must not use their knowledge to puff up themselves, but must imitate Christ's wisdom and sacrificially love one another (1 Cor. 8:1).

Colossians. At the city of Colossae, opponents of the gospel celebrated other powers, denied Christ, and shamed his followers. Paul's response is one of the most magnificent Christological confessions of the New Testament. The preexistent Son of God is set forth as the center of the universe. He is the ruler and reconciler of the whole created order; this includes all opposing forces, whether human or supernatural. This wisdom of reconciliation, which makes peace through the blood of the cross, works itself out in practical ways in the life of the church. It helps the church to persevere in times of opposition and teaches Christ's followers to be people of reconciliation. It not only subdues the cosmic powers, but reconciles Jews and Gentiles in the one body of Christ, and it forever changes relationships among believers, including slaves and masters.

Philippians. The Roman citizens of Philippi, along with the power elite of the empire, prided themselves in status and self-advancement. To help the Philippian believers live like citizens of heaven, Paul presents a hymnlike confession in which the center is the cross of Christ. It is the way of the cross that models life for believers in the world. The cross is where God's redemptive wisdom is found, and also where God manifests his own heart. Such wisdom means humility, being oriented toward others, and following the way of the cross—the divine path to exaltation and glory. This is exemplified not only in Christ's life and death, but also in Paul's life and the lives of his coworkers. Such wisdom functions in a practical way to bring the church leaders into unity.

Hebrews. The Epistle to the Hebrews was written to a community that was in danger of "falling away." The believers were struggling to move on to maturity. Persecution and discouragement were beginning to eat away at their faith. Confessing Christ is presented as the antidote to apostasy. The grand announcement of the prologue is that God has spoken to us in his Son. It appeals to believers to cling faithfully to him, in all his benefits, and to enter fully into his rest. Christ is wisdom for the Hebrews— Christ, the preexistent Son and supreme revealer of God; Christ, the incarnate Redeemer and ascended Great High Priest of the church; and Christ, the powerful ruler of the universe.

What Does Wisdom in Christ Teach Us?

The best way to grow in wisdom is, first, to meditate prayerfully and repeatedly on the New Testament's confession of Christ. Then, by God's grace and the help of the Holy Spirit, put this wisdom into practice. This is what it means to confess Christ.

Several themes constitute essential elements of the early church's confession of God's wisdom in Christ. These teachings are summarized below. Knowing these truths will help us apply God's wisdom in the varied circumstances of our own lives, and in the situations faced by our churches.

Christological Wisdom Teaches Us about God

One of the bedrock themes of New Testament Christology is that Jesus uniquely reveals God to us. The historical Jesus can do this because of his identity as the Son of God—he has a unique and intimate relationship with the Father (Matt. 11:27). The Son was sent by the Father, and came down from heaven (Gal. 4:4; Rom. 10:6). He is the Son, who from the Father's side revealed God's glory and made him known (John 1:14, 18). He is Immanuel, God with us, the Word made flesh (Matt. 1; John 1:14). Other metaphors are used as well to describe this capacity of the Son to reveal the Father. The beloved Son is confessed as "the image of the invisible God . . . in [whom] all the fullness of God was pleased to dwell" (Col. 1:15, 19). The Son is "in the form of God" and participates in "equality with God" (Phil. 2:6). The Son is the radiance of God's glory and the exact imprint of his nature (Heb. 1:3).

This motif is not merely a celebration of the deity of Christ, although it is surely that. It is also a confession that Jesus, in his unique capacity as the revealer of God, teaches us about God. He reveals to us how God exists, and shows us the ways of God. Jesus reveals to us that God exists in loving communion, not only in the Father-Son relationship but also in the eternal fellowship of the Father and the Son with the Spirit. This is how God exists, as an intimate communion of Father, Son, and Spirit. The Son teaches us about this, not only in theory but in practice. The Son cries, "Abba! Father!" and then in the hearts of believers, the Spirit echoes the same cry, "Abba! Father!"

Jesus has taught us that God's ways are counterintuitive: unlike the gods of this world, his heart is oriented toward the needs of others (Phil. 2:6–7), toward the weary and heavy laden (Matt. 11:28). If we want to know this God, Jesus can teach us about him. The Son's revelation of God's love leads naturally to the second motif.

Christological Wisdom Teaches Us about Salvation

What distinguishes God's wisdom in Christ from every other form of wisdom can be summarized in one word: the *cross*! The cross is always a dominant theme in New Testament Christological confessions. If Christ reveals God, he reveals him uniquely in his sacrificial death, and then in the resurrection. This is astonishing! We ought never to get over the wonder of it. We desperately need to imitate the way the early church, in its confession of Christ, celebrated the wisdom of the cross and explored its implications for life.

For the apostle Paul, God's wisdom is found precisely in the redemptive plan that reaches its culmination in the cross work of Christ. The only place in the New Testament where Christ is explicitly identified as the wisdom of God makes it clear that the reference is to Christ *crucified* (1 Cor. 1:23–24). The secret and hidden wisdom of God, which is now revealed, is the crucifixion of Christ (1 Cor. 2:7), with all that this means for the church and the world. Any wisdom that is not ultimately cross-oriented is not true wisdom. This is why Paul's singular "knowledge" when he came to Corinth was "Jesus Christ and him crucified" (1 Cor. 2:2). This is the nature of the wisdom that we learn in Jesus' school of discipleship (Matt. 11:29). This is what it means to "have the mind of Christ" (1 Cor. 2:16) and to have the wisdom of God revealed to us by the Spirit (1 Cor. 2:7, 10).

The cross was God's way not only of revealing himself to us but also of solving the problem of our sin and our alienation from him. Our journey through selected New Testament Christological confessions has never strayed far from this redemptive function of the cross. Here is how we find the promised rest (Matt. 11). Here is how we become children of God by a spiritual new birth (John 1:12–13). The wisdom of God in his Son is the gospel: Christ died and rose again for our sin. If we believe this and confess him as Lord, we are justified before God and experience salvation (Rom. 10:9–10). Through this work our sins are cleansed once and for all, and the ascended Son mediates for us with the Father as our perfect priest (Heb. 1:3).

This cross work redeems us from bondage, so that we might be adopted as God's children. Here we enter into the experience of the triune life revealed by the Son; by the Spirit of the Son we cry with the Son, "Abba! Father!" (Gal. 4:6).

However, it is not only our personal salvation that is wrapped up with the wisdom of the cross: the scope is cosmic. The Father is pleased through his Son to reconcile the whole created order to himself; he does this by "making peace through the blood of the cross" (Col. 1:19–20). We are personally rescued from our brokenness, but the whole created order is also destined for reconciliation: the physical order will be restored, and all people will be redeemed or brought under God's sovereign judgment. It is the cross that is at the center of this cosmic work. We saw this beautifully reflected in the confession of Philippians 2:6–11. In the end, every living being in the created order will bow and confess the lordship of God's Son (2:10–11). The cleansing from sin by the blood of the cross and the cosmic reign of Christ go together in God's wisdom. As the author of Hebrews celebrates it, after the Son cleansed our sins, he sat down at the right hand of God in anticipation of the final and complete victory over all opposition (Heb. 1:3, 13). This historical and cosmic goal of the wisdom of God in Christ points us to a third lesson that surfaced in our study.

Christological Wisdom Teaches Us about the Law

There are two fundamental and distinct ways of viewing the law of Moses. One is to see it as relatively static, serving either as a way of meriting favor with God or as a way of marking off Israel's identity by its distinctive practices (circumcision, dietary laws, the holy days). This first option manifested itself in various streams of first-century Judaism.[7] Those who followed this orientation were often zealous for God and his law. But as Paul teaches, this zeal is not according to true knowledge or wisdom (Rom. 10:2).

The second orientation is to see the law as dynamic and teleological. This view understands the law to function within a

---

7. For further study on this question, see the two volumes edited by D. A. Carson et al., *Justification and Variegated Nomism: A Fresh Appraisal of Paul and Second Temple Judaism*, vol. 1, *The Complexities of Second Temple Judaism* (Grand Rapids: Baker Academic, 2001) and *Justification and Variegated Nomism*, vol. 2, *The Paradoxes of Paul* (Grand Rapids: Baker Academic, 2004).

larger narrative framework that was anticipating fulfillment. This was the understanding of Jesus and the early church. First-century Judaism equated the law itself with wisdom—but in such a way that the law could easily turn into a burdensome yoke. Jesus and the apostolic circle understood the law to have found its intended fulfillment in the gospel, the true wisdom of the law. This orientation was reflected in a variety of ways in the Christological passages we studied.

Jesus' invitation to his disciples to take on his easy "yoke," and by implication not the burdensome weight of the law as understood by the religious leaders of the day, was a clear indication of this fulfillment motif (Matt. 11:29–30). John's prologue echoes the creation account of Genesis (John 1:1–3), refers twice to John the Baptist's preparatory ministry (1:6–8, 15), and states that Jesus came to his own people, Israel. These features all point to Jesus as the culmination of God's prior revelation. John acknowledges the law, which came through Moses, but contrasts it with the fuller revelation of grace and truth now revealed in Jesus Christ (John 1:17).

This New Testament focus on the trajectory of the law is explicit in Romans and Galatians. Christ is the "end of the law" (Rom. 10:4). The gospel is the fulfillment of Deuteronomy 30 (Rom. 10:6–8). This is why Paul says that the gospel was promised through the prophets in the Holy Scriptures (1:2), and that the righteousness of God is now revealed "apart from the law" and yet supported by "the Law and the Prophets" (3:21). For Paul, the law is understood along a historical trajectory. For Gentiles to return to life under the law, from a period that was now surpassed by the "fullness of time," would be foolish. The Son came "to redeem those who were under the law" and bring freedom (Gal. 4:4; 5:1). James captures the essence of this orientation when he calls the law "the perfect law, the law of liberty" (James 1:25).

In the prologue to Hebrews, the former revelation is understood along this same goal-oriented trajectory. God spoke earlier to our spiritual ancestors by the prophets, and the law was mediated by angels, but now in these last days he has spoken in his

Son (Heb. 1:1, 4). Later in his epistle, the author will speak of the law and its fulfillment in Christ as analogous to shadow and substance (10:1).

One of the most important entailments of this prophetic orientation to the law is God's purpose of including rather than excluding all people in his redemptive purposes. Hidden in the Old Testament, but now revealed, was the "mystery" that the Gentiles, as well as the Jews, would be included in the people of God (Col. 2:27). In the church, with both Jews and Gentiles reconciled to God, the wonderful wisdom of God is made known (Eph. 3:6, 9–10). This motif is an important reminder to us of both the Jewish nature of the gospel, with its roots in the Old Testament, and its cosmic intent, that all the nations of the earth would be blessed through the seed of Abraham (Gen. 12:3). The wisdom of God in Christ brings hope to the whole world. "Torah" or the law of Moses may have appeared ethnic and burdensome, but in the wisdom of God its fulfillment in Christ would bring true righteousness and spiritual freedom to all people.

Christological Wisdom Teaches Us How to Live as the Community of Faith

Christology and ecclesiology are inseparable; while our study has been primarily about Christ, it has also been about the body of Christ. The wisdom of God, as we have seen, is uniquely embodied in the person and work of Christ. But as a consequence of his work and the continuing ministry of his Spirit, that wisdom is now lived out in the body of Christ (Eph. 3:10). The way we live is a reflection of the wisdom that shapes us. God's wisdom in Christ calls us first to *be* a radically different people and then to *act* out of that identity—to model an alternative way of being in the world.

What kind of people does the Christology of the New Testament call us to be? We saw that Christ's capacity to reveal God's wisdom is directly related to his identity as the Son. In the same way, one of the persistent themes describing our identity as participants in Christ's wisdom relates to our status as children. This surprising motif is found in nearly every text we examined. The Father reveals wisdom to little children (Matt. 11:25). Those who receive the Word are given the right to become children of God, and are born of God (John 1:12–13). The Father sent the Son so that believers might receive adoption as sons, and be sons (Gal. 4:5, 7). Other elements likewise contribute to the dominance of this sonship theme: for example, God is our Father, we are brothers and sisters, and we share in the inheritance of the Son.

We must resist our modern cultural tendency to read this filial relationship in an overly individualistic way. We all come to faith in Christ as unique persons, with our own special identities. But as we are born of God, we immediately become part of the community of faith, constituted by the Spirit into the body of Christ. To live in the wisdom of Christ is to live in community as brothers and sisters, reflecting the fellowship of the triune God.

Nothing determines our identity more than family. This is what makes the metaphor of sonship so powerful. To be God's children means that we are responsive, teachable, and obedient to our Father's wisdom. It also means that we can rest in our relationship with the Father, as his children who are forgiven (Col. 1:13–14), righteous in Christ (Rom. 10:9–10), freed from bondage (Gal. 4:5; 5:1), and heirs of all things (Gal. 4:7). It means that we can enjoy deep intimacy with God and together cry, "Abba! Father!" by the Spirit of his Son (Gal. 4:6).

As God's children, we reflect his wisdom in the world. Who we *are* determines how we act. After confessing Christ as the model for our way of life, Paul challenges us to actually be "children of God" in the world (Phil. 2:15; cf. 1 John 3:1–3).

The Epistle of James, with its subtle Christological wisdom, puts it this way: "Who is wise and understanding among you? By his good conduct let him show his works in the meekness of wisdom" (James 3:13).[8] Paul prays that we will be filled with

---

8. For a helpful study on wisdom and the life of the church in James, see Christopher W. Morgan, *A Theology of James: Wisdom for God's People* (Phillipsburg, NJ: P&R Publishing, 2010).

wisdom, so as to walk in a manner worthy of the Lord (Col. 1:9; Phil. 1:27). So how do we live out our identity as God's children in the world? What should this look like to those who observe us? We have caught some important glimpses in our study. Here are three of the more important lessons.

Living in Wisdom Means Having a Humble Spirit. The school of Christ's wisdom teaches us that the indispensable condition for true greatness is humility. This is why the incarnate Son of God described himself as "gentle and lowly in heart" (Matt. 11:28). James understood this when he characterized the believer's conduct as stemming from "the meekness of wisdom." How contrary to the wisdom that is from below, which is marked by "jealousy and selfish ambition." If we seek social status and exploit our rights for selfish advantage, "this is not the wisdom that comes down from above, but is earthly, unspiritual, demonic" (James 3:13–16).

The incredible insight that Paul reveals in Philippians is that this heavenly humility is a reflection of God's own greatness: God, in the person of his Son, did not exploit his rights, but humbled himself for the sake of others (Phil. 2:6–8). A person who has learned well under Jesus' yoke will reflect a similar gentle and humble spirit. The virtue of humility can come only from being rightly related to the Father, and living obediently under the all-sufficient lordship of Christ. When the church loses this humility, it is a denial of Christ and his wisdom—making it impossible for her to faithfully fulfill her mission in the world.

Living in Wisdom Means Suffering for Others. When Christ invited people to be his disciples and to enter into his school of wisdom (Matt. 11:28–29), he knew this would lead them to the cross. This is implied when Jesus reminded his disciples, "Whoever does not take his cross and follow me is not worthy of me" (Matt. 10:38), and "If anyone would come after me, let him deny himself and take up his cross and follow me" (Matt. 16:24). While only Christ could die for our sins, the Christian life is also a "cruciform" life, one shaped by the way of the cross. Paul, before confessing Christ's example (Phil. 2:6–11), wrote that "it has been granted to you that for the sake of Christ you should not only believe in him but also suffer for his sake" (Phil. 1:29). Then Paul placed "the death of the cross" at the very center of his Christological confession. Christ humbled himself and became obedient unto death, even the death of the cross. We are called, in Christian wisdom, to follow this same path. What does this look like?

People who live in the self-sacrificing way of the cross become oriented toward the needs of others, even at great cost to themselves. This is the wisdom from above that is "full of mercy and good fruits" (James 3:17). People trained in it will take the gospel to the ends of the earth so that others might know the saving benefits of Christ. In a world marred by evil and violence, they will spend their own lives as expressions of love to meet the desperate needs of people everywhere. They will do this with joy, knowing that in the way of the cross God's wisdom and power are made known.

Living in Wisdom Means Pursuing Peace and Reconciliation. The violent animosity of a fallen world is what makes humility and the way of the cross so costly. God's mission in Christ, and therefore the mission of the church, aims directly at this opposition.

Therefore, the people taught in the school of Christ must be a community of peace and reconciliation: any other way of life is a contradiction. James captures this motif for us when he argues that the wisdom from above is first pure, then "peaceable," and that "a harvest of righteousness is sown in peace by those who make peace" (James 3:17–18).

People who have true wisdom seek the peace and welfare of others over their own rights (1 Cor. 8:1–13). The wisdom of the cross brings Jews and Gentiles together, removing the hostility between them (Ephesians, Colossians). It brings a master and slave together on new terms of identity in Christ (Col. 1, Philemon). It brings church leaders together (Phil. 4:2–3). This is why selfish and worldly divisions in the church are such a blemish on the gospel: they are a blatant denial of God's wisdom found in the cross of Christ (1 Cor. 1). If the Christian community cannot learn to live at peace in the wisdom of Christ, how can she hope to be an agent of peace and reconciliation in the world? If you and I are not peacemakers, how can we claim to be taught in the school of Christ?

Why Seek Wisdom in Christ?

Why do we need a wisdom that is Christ-centered and shaped by the cross? The answer relates to God's own heart and our good. The Father delights in the Son and calls us to do the same. The Son reflects the Father's glory and enables us to share in this glory. But God's wisdom is not only Christ-centered; it is also cross-shaped. When God, in the person of his Son, took on human nature, he revealed himself as one who was oriented toward the needs of others. This supreme act of love accomplished our salvation through the cross, and taught us how to live in this same self-sacrificing way. Jesus invites us to come and find rest and satisfaction in him, but also to come and take his way of life, his yoke, as our own wisdom.

God's wisdom has always called out with an invitation that demands a response (Prov. 1:20; 8:1). It calls out to us today in the person and work of Christ.

Perhaps there is no better way to conclude this study than to quote James, the Lord's brother, and then Jesus himself:

> If any of you lacks wisdom, let him ask God, who gives generously to all without reproach, and it will be given him. (James 1:5)

> Come to me, all who labor and are heavy laden, and I will give you rest. Take my yoke upon you, and learn from me, for I am gentle and lowly in heart, and you will find rest for your souls. (Matt. 11:28–29)

Questions for Study and Reflection

Introduction: The Need for Wisdom

1. The wisdom of the world puts pressure on the church to conform to its ways. Can you think of some contemporary examples that illustrate this?

2. There are many ways to approach the study of Christ, such as his two natures, his person and work, or his titles (Lord, Savior, Lamb of God). Summarize the approach that this study will take to the study of Christology.

3. Summarize the more important features of wisdom found in the Old Testament.

4. What is the essential difference between God's wisdom in Christ (i.e., "Christological wisdom") and the best wisdom of philosophy?

5. In what ways is Christ different from "Lady Wisdom" as she is understood in Jewish literature?

6. What are the dangers mentioned in the warning at the end of this chapter? How can we best avoid these pitfalls?

Chapter 1—An Invitation to Follow Jesus (Matthew 11:25-30)

1. Why is the invitation to Jesus' school of wisdom described as "dangerous"? List and discuss how following Christ and his teachings might be dangerous for you.

191

2. Matthew 11:25–30 refers indirectly to wisdom. What is this wisdom? Try to list three or four things that characterize it.

3. How did Solomon's wisdom and Jonah's preaching relate to Gentiles? How does this relate to God's wisdom in Christ?

4. Jesus invites us to take his "yoke" upon us. How did the yoke relate to wisdom in first-century Judaism (e.g., Sir. 51:23–26)? What kinds of yokes do people take on today as sources of wisdom?

5. The Jews found wisdom in the Mosaic law. What shift of interpretation takes place with the coming of Christ? Where is wisdom now found?

6. What are the "learning outcomes" and the "curriculum" in Christ's school of wisdom?

Chapter 2—An Invitation to Receive the Word (John 1:1–18)

1. Some say John's Gospel is for evangelism and others say it is intended for the training of disciples in the church. How do you think his book functions and why?

2. In what ways are John's prologue and Jesus' invitation to discipleship in Matthew 11 alike? Try to list three or four similarities.

3. Several of the ways in which Jesus is distinct from Lady Wisdom are also arguments for the full deity of Christ. What are several of these distinctions?

4. Why does John identify the Word with the work of creation? What does he emphasize by doing this?

5. What does the "glory" of the Son refer to in John's prologue? How is this different from how we typically think of God's glory?

6. List some practical ways that we can live out God's wisdom in Christ through our lives together in the church.

Chapter 3—Wisdom and the Crucified Christ
(1 Corinthians 1:18-24, 30-31; 8:6)

1. Have you experienced serious divisiveness in the church, or even a church split? How might true wisdom have remedied the situation?

2. While Paul uses "wisdom" in two negative ways (worldly thinking, mere eloquence), he also uses the term in positive ways. What are some features of this Christian wisdom found in Ephesians and Colossians? Cite the references.

3. When the apostle calls Christ "the wisdom of God" in 1 Corinthians 1:24, what exactly is this wisdom? Support your answer from the context of 1 Corinthians.

4. Acquiring God's wisdom can seem like an overwhelming challenge, especially in view of the countervoices in the culture all around us. What role does the Holy Spirit play in helping us to know God's wisdom in Christ?

5. How is Paul's confession of Christ in 1 Corinthians 8:6—an important text for the deity of Christ—actually used for an ethical purpose? At Corinth, this related to treating a fellow Christian properly over the issue of meat offered to idols. How might we apply this insight to Christian relationships today?

6. What are the three themes around which God's wisdom in Christ can be organized? What are some practical lessons we have learned from each of these themes?

Chapter 4—Wisdom and the Cosmic Christ
(Colossians 1:15-20)

1. What kinds of powers would you say are most threatening to believers and the church today?

2. How are contemporary doctrinal errors similar to or different from the type of error that Paul describes at Colossae?

3. Paul places Christ, God's Son, at the center of his literary structure in Colossians 1:15–20, and at the center of his life and theology. In what ways do you struggle to keep Christ as the exclusive center of your life and thought?

4. How does Christ relate to the created order, according to this passage? What implications might this have for how Christians view such issues as the environment and treatment of the human body?

5. What is surprising about the way Paul introduces the church in Colossians 1:18? How does this make your local church significant?

6. How does our personal participation in God's wonderful reconciliation in Christ lead us also to participate in God's larger work of reconciliation in the world around us? Think of Paul's intervention for the slave Onesimus in the Epistle of Philemon. Can you give some other real-life examples?

Chapter 5—Wisdom and the Way of the Cross (Philippians 2:5–11)

1. What are some of the cultural practices or patterns of thinking that influence the church today, but are contrary to wisdom in Christ? What are some that you find particularly influential in your life?

2. How does early Christian worship through music relate to God's wisdom in Christ? How might this help us constructively evaluate our music in the church today?

3. What questions are typically asked of Philippians 2:5–11, and what question does our study ask of the text?

4. What is the astonishing truth about what God is like that is revealed by Christ? How might this change the way you live as God's child, being conformed to his likeness in Christ?

5. The way of the cross was contrary to the status-seeking values of the imperial city of Philippi. What are some specific ways that our culture is status-oriented (both outside and inside the church)? How might we live differently to reflect the pattern of wisdom Jesus shows us?

6. Christ, Paul, and the apostle's coworkers all provided examples of "wisdom living." Can you cite some contemporary examples of Christians who have modeled "the way of the cross"?

Chapter 6—Wisdom and the Priesthood of Christ (Hebrews 1:1–4)

1. Can you think of a crisis in your life or the life of your church that made following Christ difficult?

2. We have seen several passages about Christ that have exhibited intricate and artistic literary structures (Phil. 2; Col. 1; and now Heb. 1). Why do you think the authors present their Christology in this fashion?

3. Both the literary structure of the prologue to the Hebrews and the sentence's grammatical core stress God's revelation in his Son. What specific arguments for Christ's superior revelation are contained in these verses?

4. One of the unique contributions of Hebrews to New Testament theology is the identification of Jesus' unique priesthood. How is this important doctrine situated in the prologue (Heb. 1:1–4)? How does the prologue illustrate the apostolic pattern of applying Christology to the needs of the church?

5. One of the arguments of the Epistle to the Hebrews is that the persons (e.g., Moses) and institutions (e.g., the tabernacle)

of the Old Testament were good, but Jesus is better. List some ways in which Jesus as the Son could be described as superior to "Lady Wisdom."

6. The major themes of God's wisdom in Christ revolve around revelation, creation, and redemption—or Jesus as prophet, king, and priest. How are these roles reflected in the life of the church as she follows in the wisdom of Christ?

Conclusion: Learning to Live in the Wisdom of Christ

1. Can you identify some areas in contemporary life where there seems to be an excess of knowledge, but a shortfall of wisdom?

2. The strongest conceptual link between Christ and Lady Wisdom is how each is portrayed in the Bible as playing a role in creation. List the four ways that Christ's creation role exceeds that of Wisdom.

3. After reading the review of the Christological wisdom applied in each of the passages we have studied, select the text that was the most meaningful for you. In what way did you find the passage significant?

4. One of the bedrock themes of New Testament Christology is the way Christ reveals God. As a result of our study, can you list two or three of the characteristics of God that are uniquely revealed by Jesus?

5. Summarize in your own words how the cross is at the center of God's wisdom in Christ.

6. What are the three characteristics that should be true of a community that is shaped by Christological wisdom? Can you give real-life examples of people or local churches that have embodied these qualities?

Select Resources on
Christ and Wisdom

(*Advanced Students)

General Resources

*Barton, Stephen C., ed. *Where Shall Wisdom Be Found? Wisdom in the Bible, the Church and the Contemporary World*. Edinburgh: T&T Clark, 1999.

*Ebert, Daniel. "Wisdom in New Testament Christology, with Special Reference to Hebrews 1:1–4." PhD diss., Trinity Evangelical Divinity School, 1998.

*Greene, Colin J. D. *Christology in Cultural Perspective: Marking Out the Horizons*. Grand Rapids: Eerdmans, 2004.

Gunton, Colin. "Christ, the Wisdom of God: A Study in Divine and Human Action." In *Where Shall Wisdom Be Found? Wisdom in the Bible, the Church and the Contemporary World*, edited by Stephen C. Barton, 249–61. Edinburgh: T&T Clark, 1999.

Longenecker, Richard N., ed. *Contours of Christology in the New Testament*. Grand Rapids: Eerdmans, 2005.

Treier, Daniel. "Wisdom." In *Dictionary for Theological Interpretation of the Bible*, edited by Kevin Vanhoozer, 844–47. Grand Rapids: Baker Academic, 2005.

Resources on Biblical Passages

WISDOM IN THE OLD TESTAMENT

*Crenshaw, James L. *Old Testament Wisdom: An Introduction*. 3rd ed. Louisville: Westminster/John Knox Press, 2010.

Estes, Daniel J. *Handbook on the Wisdom Books and Psalms: Job, Psalms, Proverbs, Ecclesiastes, Song of Songs*. Grand Rapids: Baker Academic, 2010.

WISDOM IN THE GOSPELS

Barton, Stephen C. "Gospel Wisdom." In *Where Shall Wisdom Be Found? Wisdom in the Bible, the Church and the Contemporary World*, edited by Stephen C. Barton, 93–110. Edinburgh: T&T Clark, 1999.

Gathercole, Simon J. *The Preexistent Son: Recovering the Christologies of Matthew, Mark, and Luke*. Grand Rapids: Eerdmans, 2006. Especially 193–209 for critique of Wisdom Christology in the Gospels.

*Macaskill, Grant. *Revealed Wisdom and Inaugurated Eschatology in Ancient Judaism and Early Christianity*. Supplements to *Journal for the Study of Judaism*, vol. 115. Boston: Brill, 2007. Especially chap. 4.

McDonough, Sean H. *Christ as Creator: Origins of a New Testament Doctrine*. New York: Oxford University Press, 2009. Especially 37–40.

WISDOM IN THE EPISTLES

Fee, Gordon D. *Pauline Christology: An Exegetical-Theological Study*. Peabody, MA: Hendrickson, 2008. Especially Appendix A: "Christ and Personified Wisdom," 595–630; also 102–5, 186–87, 317–25.

Hays, Richard B. "Wisdom according to Paul." In *Where Shall Wisdom Be Found? Wisdom in the Bible, the Church and the Contemporary World*, edited by Stephen C. Barton, 111–23. Edinburgh: T&T Clark, 1999.

Resources on Special Topics

CHRIST HYMNS

*Hengel, Martin. "The Song about Christ in Earliest Worship." In his *Studies in Early Christology*, translated by Rollins Kearns, 227–91. Edinburgh: T&T Clark, 1995.

Karris, Robert J. *A Symphony of New Testament Hymns*. Collegeville, MN: Liturgical Press, 1996.

*Martin, Ralph P., and Brian J. Dodd, eds. *Where Christology Began: Essays on Philippians 2*. Louisville: Westminster/John Knox Press, 1998.

CHRIST'S ROLE AS CREATOR

McDonough, Sean H. *Christ as Creator: Origins of a New Testament Doctrine*. New York: Oxford University Press, 2009.

DEITY OF CHRIST AND WISDOM

Bauckham, Richard. *Jesus and the God of Israel: God Crucified and Other Studies on the New Testament's Christology of Divine Identity*. Grand Rapids: Eerdmans, 2009.

Dunn, James D. G. *Did the First Christians Worship Jesus? The New Testament Evidence*. Louisville: Westminster/John Knox Press, 2010. Especially 72–84, 116–129.

Hurtado, Larry W. *How on Earth Did Jesus Become a God? Historical Questions about Earliest Devotion to Jesus*. Grand Rapids: Eerdmans, 2005.

JESUS AS TEACHER OF WISDOM OR SAGE

*Hengel, Martin. "Jesus as Messianic Teacher of Wisdom and the Beginnings of Christology." In his *Studies in Early Christology*, translated by Rollins Kearns, 73–117. Edinburgh: T&T Clark, 1995.

Witherington, Ben, III. *Jesus the Sage: The Pilgrimage of Wisdom*. Minneapolis: Fortress Press, 1994.

LADY WISDOM

*Good, Deirdre J. *Reconstructing the Tradition of Sophia in Gnostic Literature*. Society of Biblical Literature Monograph ser. 32. Atlanta: Scholars Press, 1987.

Murphy, Roland E. *The Tree of Life: An Exploration of Biblical Wisdom Literature*. 3rd ed. Grand Rapids: Eerdmans, 2002. Especially chap. 9, "Lady Wisdom," 133–49; see also 227–29; 278–81.

WISDOM AND THE LAW

*Schnabel, Eckhard J. *Law and Wisdom from Ben Sira to Paul: A Tradition Historical Enquiry into the Relation of Law, Wisdom, and Ethics*. 16 vols. Tübingen: Mohr Siebeck, 1985.

Theology and Wisdom

*Ford, David. *Christian Wisdom: Desiring God and Learning in Love*. Cambridge: Cambridge University Press, 2007.

*Ford, David, and Graham Stanton. *Reading Texts, Seeking Wisdom: Scripture and Theology*. Grand Rapids: Eerdmans, 2004.

*O'Boyle, Aidan. *Towards a Contemporary Wisdom Christology: Some Catholic Christologies in German, English and French, 1965–1995*. 98 vols. Roma: Editrice Pontificia Università Gregoriana, 2003.

Treier, Daniel J. *Virtue and the Voice of God: Toward Theology as Wisdom*. Grand Rapids: Eerdmans, 2006.

Index of Scripture and Extrabiblical References

201

Index of Subjects and Names